FROM THE BIBLE-TEACHING MINISTRY OF

CHARLES R. SWINDOLL

INSIGHT'S
BIBLE
Handbook

PRACTICAL HELPS FOR BIBLE STUDY

INSIGHT FOR LIVING

INSIGHT'S BIBLE HANDBOOK

From the Bible-Teaching Ministry of Charles R. Swindoll and Insight for Living

Charles R. Swindoll has devoted his life to the clear, practical teaching and application of God's Word and His grace. Chuck currently is the senior pastor of Stonebriar Community Church in Frisco, Texas; but his listening audience extends far beyond this local church body. As a leading program in Christian broadcasting, *Insight for Living* airs in major Christian radio markets around the world, reaching people groups in languages they can understand. Chuck's extensive writing ministry has also served the body of Christ worldwide and his leadership as president and now chancellor of Dallas Theological Seminary has helped prepare and equip a new generation for ministry.

Published By:
IFL Publishing House
A Division of Insight for Living
Post Office Box 251007
Plano, Texas 75025-1007

Writing Contributors:
John Adair, Th.M., Ph.D. candidate, Dallas Theological Seminary
Derrick G. Jeter, Th.M., Dallas Theological Seminary
Wil Luce, Certificate of Graduation, Dallas Theological Seminary
Barb Peil, M.A., Christian Education, Dallas Theological Seminary
Wendy Peterson, B.A., California State University at Fullerton
Wayne Stiles, Th.M., D.Min., Dallas Theological Seminary
Michael J. Svigel, Th.M., Ph.D., Dallas Theological Seminary

Editor in Chief: Cynthia Swindoll, President, Insight for Living
Executive Vice President: Wayne Stiles, Th.M., D.Min., Dallas Theological Seminary
Editor: Brie Engeler, M.A., Biblical Studies, Dallas Theological Seminary
Copy Editors: Jim Craft, M.A., English, Mississippi College
Melanie Munnell, M.A., Humanities, The University of Texas at Dallas
Project Supervisor, Creative Ministries: Cari Harris, B.A., Journalism, Grand Canyon University
Project Coordinator, Communications: Dusty R. Crosby, B.S., Communications, Dallas Baptist University
Proofreader: Joni Halpin, B.S., Accountancy, Miami University
Cover Designer: Steven Tomlin, Embry-Riddle Aeronautical University, 1992–1995
Production Artist: Nancy Gustine, B.F.A., Advertising Art, University of North Texas
Cover Image: Copyright © 2007 by iStockphoto.com.

ISBN: 978-1-57972-758-1
Printed in the United States of America

TABLE OF CONTENTS

HOW TO STUDY THE BIBLE

APPENDIX

A NOTE FROM CHUCK SWINDOLL

In our tolerant, postmodern world, what is our final authority?

This foundational question must be answered by all of us. Where do we go for a clear understanding of right and wrong? Where do we turn for guidance when we encounter difficult decisions, cultural pressures, and times of personal crisis? What source can we consult for the truth about who God is, who we are, and how He has bridged the distance between us?

Make no mistake about it . . . God's Word, the Bible, is our final authority for faith and practice. It is living, infallible truth from our living, infallible God. Knowing and loving Him means knowing and loving His Word.

God didn't simply *think* His message. He didn't simply *speak* His message, reveal it in the clouds, or communicate it through dreams and visions to people in biblical times. No, He saw to it that His Word was actually written down by His prophets and apostles, then preserved and translated through the ages by carefully selected, faithful followers. He communicated it in clear, understandable terms, so people in all generations could read it, grasp its significance, and be transformed by it. There is no book of wisdom, science, history, or poetry like the Bible—it is *God's very Word.*

Because God felt it was so important to give us His Word, we should take the time to read it, to study it, and to allow it to speak to us and change us.

With *Insight's Bible Handbook*, you will discover the *who, what, where, when, why,* and *how* of the Bible.

- *Who* wrote it and preserved it for us?
- *What* does it mean?
- *Where* did it come from, and how did it get to us?
- *When* was it written?
- *Why* should we trust it?
- *How* do we understand and apply it today?

You'll learn how neglected subjects like history and geography can help you trust and understand the Bible. You'll discover how to do meaningful Bible studies, including topical and biographical approaches, and even glean some tips on how to teach God's Word to others.

I hope that this Bible handbook will equip you to dig deeper into the Scriptures, which will provide lasting guidance and encouragement on your spiritual journey.

Charles R. Swindoll

INSIGHT'S
BIBLE
Handbook

BACKGROUNDS
OF THE *Bible*

HOW FIRM A FOUNDATIC

Why We Have Confidence in the Bibl.

by Charles R. Swindoll

What is your final authority in life? I mean, when you're cornered, when you're really up against it, when you're forced to face reality, upon what do you lean?

Before you answer too quickly, think about it for a few moments. When it comes to establishing a standard for morality, what's your guide? When you need an ethical compass to find your way out of an ethical jungle, where's north? When you're on a stormy, churning sea of emotions, which lighthouse shows you where to find the shore?

There can be no more reliable authority on earth than God's Word, the Bible. This timeless, trustworthy source of truth holds the key that unlocks life's mysteries. It alone provides us with the shelter we need in times of storm.

But we need to understand why. Why does this Book qualify as our final authority?

God's Word Is Truth

"Your word is truth," Jesus said as He prayed to the Father (John 17:17). Truth, real truth, truth you can rely on, truth that will never shrivel up or turn sour, truth that will never backfire or mislead—that's the truth in the Bible. That is what the Bible is about. That is why the Bible provides us with *the* constant and *the* needed support.

God's Book Is God's Voice

Scripture is God's message. It is, in fact, God's Word. The apostle Paul testified clearly to that truth in his first letter to the Thessalonians:

> ...iis reason we also constantly thank God that when
> ...a received the word of God which you heard from us,
> ...ou accepted it not as the word of men, but for what it
> really is, the word of God, which also performs its work
> in you who believe. (1 Thessalonians 2:13)

Think of it this way: God's Book is, as it were, God's voice. If our Lord were to make Himself visible and return to earth and speak His message, it would be in keeping with the Bible. His message of truth would tie in exactly with what you see in Scripture—His opinion, His counsel, His commands, His desires, His warnings, His very heart, His very mind. When you rely on God's voice, His very message, you have a sure foundation; you have truth that can be trusted; you have power that imparts new life and releases grace by which you can grow in faith and commitment.

God's Word Will Endure

Do you realize there are only two eternal things on earth today? Only two: people and God's Word. Everything else will ultimately be burned up—everything else. Kind of sets your priorities straight, doesn't it? The stuff we place on the shelf, the things we put frames around, the trophies and whatnots we shine and love to show off, the things we're so proud of—it's all headed for the final bonfire (2 Peter 3:7, 10–12). But not God's Book! Peter reminds us that the truth "stands forever" (1 Peter 1:25 NIV). Grass will grow and then it will wither; flowers will bloom and then they will die. But God's written message, the truth, will abide forever. All His promises will be fulfilled; His redemptive truth cannot be annulled or changed; His powerful Word will accomplish what He desires and will achieve the purpose for which He sent it (Isaiah 55:10–11). His Word will endure!

God's Word Is Inspired

But wait. Doesn't all this talk about the Bible lead to an important question that must be asked? The question goes like this: How can anyone get so excited about something that was written by men? We have no problem with the Giver of truth. He gave it . . . but wasn't the corrupted when He relayed it to earth through the hands and m. sinful men?

This is the perfect moment for you to become acquainted with three doctrinal terms: *revelation, inspiration*, and *illumination. Revelation* occurred when God gave His truth. *Inspiration* occurred when the writers of Scripture received and recorded His truth. Today, when we understand and apply His truth, that's *illumination.*

The critical issue — your confidence in the Bible — is directly related to your confidence in its inspiration. How then can we be sure that God's Word is free from error, absolutely true, and therefore deserving of our complete trust? Paul provides great help in answering this question:

> All Scripture is inspired by God and profitable for teaching, for reproof, for correction, for training in righteousness; so that the man of God may be adequate, equipped for every good work. (2 Timothy 3:16–17)

When God revealed His truth for human writers to record, He "breathed out" His Word. When we dictate a letter to someone, we "breathe out" a message and someone else types what we've said. But did the writers of Scripture simply take dictation?

If you know much about the Bible, you realize that it was written by many different people with many different personalities. Peter doesn't sound like John; John doesn't sound like David. Somehow each writer's personality was preserved without corrupting the text with human weakness and error. That rules out the idea of dictation.

So how did God cause this to happen? Second Peter 1:21 gives us a further clue: "For prophecy never had its origin in the will of man, but men spoke from God as they were carried along by the Holy Spirit" (NIV).

The English phrase "carried along" is translated from an ancient Greek nautical term (*pherō*) describing ships at sea. When a ship was at the mercy of the winds, waves, and currents of the sea, it was "carried along" apart from its own power. That's the word used here. They raised,

their sails, the Holy Spirit filled them, and they were "carried
the direction He desired.

s Word Will Hold You Up

our conclusion is this: In the Bible we have the preservation of a completely dependable, authoritative, inspired text. The question each of us
must ask ourselves is this: Can I rely on it, especially when I go through
those chaotic experiences in life? My answer, and I pray it is your answer,
is this: absolutely and unreservedly! The wonderful thing about relying
on God's Book is that it gives you stability. It gives you that deep sense of
purpose and meaning. No other counsel will get you through the long
haul. No other truth will help you stand firm in the storms of doubt
and uncertainty. No other reality will give you strength for each day and
deep hope for tomorrow. No other instruction has the power to give new
meaning to your life.[1]

FASCINATING FACTS

- Some pyramids had already been built in Egypt when Joseph arrived.

- The Temple of Artemis (Diana) in Ephesus was one of the Seven Wonders of the World. It was built of white marble and covered with gold and jewels.

- The Great Wall of China was built and the Mayan calendar was invented two hundred years before Jesus was born.

- The apostle Paul never saw the Coliseum in Rome. The building project began four years after his death.

- Daniel, Confucius, and Buddha all lived in the same era.

- Jonah was sent to Nineveh, which is in modern-day Iraq.

- Queen Esther, whose story is told in the Old Testament book of Esther, and the Greek philosopher Socrates lived in the same century.

- Queen Esther's throne was in ancient Susa, which was about one hundred miles from modern Kuwait City, Kuwait.

- King David predated the first Olympic Games in Greece by about two hundred years.

- Cleopatra, Queen of Egypt, died about thirty years before Jesus was born.

"BIBLE WANNABES"
True and False Scriptures

by Michael J. Svigel

In the AD 200s, groups known as Gnostics added dozens of mystical and mythical documents to their "scriptures." Then, in the 600s, Muslims touted the Quran as the final, superior addition to God's holy writings. In the mid 1500s, the Roman Catholic Church declared the writings of the Apocrypha to be on par with the rest of inspired Scripture. And in the early 1800s, Joseph Smith published the Book of Mormon as "another" testament of Jesus Christ.

Why don't Christians believe that the additions of the Gnostics, the Muslims, the Catholics of the Middle Ages, or the Mormons belong in our Bibles?

The Real Bible versus "Bible Wannabes"

During the early years of the Christian church, many "Bible wannabes" competed for acceptance. Titles like the Gospel of Thomas, the Apocryphon of John, the Gospel of Truth, and the recently discovered Gospel of Judas all presented different portrayals of Christ and different versions of Christianity. Why aren't some of these rejected writings found in our New Testament? More importantly, how did the early Christians choose the books we have in our Bibles today?

Some misled or misinformed people believe that a council of bishops at Nicaea in AD 325 voted on these particular books out of hundreds of worthy competitors. And some misguided historians today say that early church leaders selected only writings that reinforced their authority and rejected any that challenged it. The canonicity of the books of the Bible is an important issue. (The Greek word for *canon*, in this context, refers to a "rule" or "standard.") Clearly, understanding the difference between authentic Scripture and "Bible wannabes" will help strengthen our confidence that the Bible we hold in our hands contains only the books that

...g . . . and none that don't. To answer the question of how the
...v Testament books became part of the canon of Scripture, we need to
...vel back in time to the earliest days of the church — *before* Christians
...ad a complete collection of Bible books.

Scripture in the Early Church

For the earliest Christians, Scripture consisted of the Old Testament
books as we have them in our Bibles today. Writing and circulating the
collection of New Testament writings took some time. How did this occur?
How did the early Christians know which books were Bible-worthy
and which were "Bible wannabes"? Can we trust their judgment in this
important matter?

The fact is, the authority of any New Testament writing was not
dependent on one man's decision, the vote of a council, or affirmation
by a creed. A particular book's canonicity depended upon whether or
not it came from the pen of a true apostle or prophet inspired by the
Holy Spirit. Other writings could be true, beneficial, and edifying . . . but
not inspired and inerrant.

So how did early Christians know whether a book or letter had been
written by an apostle or prophet? In the same way you and I can tell
whether a letter we receive is from a close friend or from a total stranger,
early Christians knew which books were authentic because they person-
ally knew the authors. The Christian leaders and communities to whom
the apostles and prophets originally wrote knew which books were
authentic (written by a true apostle or prophet), *true* (the information in
the book was reliable), and therefore *authoritative* (God's inspired words).
Almost immediately these authentic, true, and authoritative writings
began to be copied and passed around to other churches. From the start,
churches used these writings for instruction and worship. So for most
New Testament books, there was little question about whether or not
they were canonical — worthy for use in the faith and practice of the
churches.

But wouldn't later generations lose their certainty about those writings and be fooled by "Bible wannabes"? No, the Christian churches

still knew which writings were true and which were false. For example around AD 95 the apostle John may have handed a copy of his Gospel over to Onesimus, pastor of the church in Ephesus, who then sent copie to Polycarp in nearby Smyrna around AD 100, who then gave a copy to his student Irenaeus around AD 150, and so on. At no time would these believers have questioned whether or not John wrote this book. Its place in the life and worship of the original churches was already firmly established. And eventually, remote Christians in other churches and regions would also come to accept the Gospel of John as they researched its history, examined its content, and corresponded with other churches. This specific example regarding John's Gospel can be applied to other New Testament writings as well.

Even when we hear about "disputed" books that took a little longer for all the churches to accept (or reject), we should actually be *encouraged* by this news rather than discouraged. Why? Because this prudence indicates that the early church leaders were extremely cautious regarding writings about which they were uncertain. They diligently investigated these writings to discover the truth before they reached universal agreement on what should be accepted as true Scripture.

The Whole Bible and Nothing More

Although the majority of our New Testament books were collected and used together throughout the churches by about AD 200, an official affirmation of our present New Testament did not occur until the Council of Carthage in AD 397. Their New Testament canon is the same as that accepted by the Protestant churches and evangelicals today. Again, the council did not vote on these books from among dozens of competing "candidates" for Scripture; rather, it acknowledged the writings that Christians all over the world had already accepted by that time—and have used ever since.

So do the Book of Mormon, the Apocrypha, the Quran, and the Gnostic gospels belong in our Bibles? No! We can be confident that, by the wisdom and providence of God, the early church made sure that the book we trust as inspired Scripture contains the *whole* Bible and *nothing more.*

DEFINITIONS OF ANCIENT WRITINGS

Canonical Writings	These writings of the Old and New Testaments were accepted by Jesus, the apostles, and the early Christians as inspired by the Spirit. They were written by apostles or prophets without doctrinal or factual error. Christians believe the last books of the New Testament were written by AD 100. The Protestant list of canonical books includes sixty-six total writings—thirty-nine Old Testament books and twenty-seven New Testament books.
Apocrypha and Pseudepigrapha	These writings were not universally regarded as canonical. Some of these claimed to have been written by famous Old and New Testament personalities but were later determined to be forgeries (*pseudepigrapha* means "false writings"). Occasionally, early Christians accepted a few of these writings as authentic—especially if they contained passages that supported their theology. But in the process of *canonization*—affirming the truly inspired writings—apocryphal and pseudepigraphal writings were eventually rejected.
The Masoretic Text	This version of the Hebrew Old Testament is most commonly used by both Christian and Jewish biblical scholars for study and translation. This version is characterized by *Masora*, or traditional vowel and reading symbols added around the all-consonant Hebrew text to help in pronunciation and oral reading. The work of the Masoretes—those Jewish scribes who copied and preserved the Hebrew Bible—started about AD 500. Except for the Dead Sea Scrolls, the various manuscripts of the Masoretic text are the only versions of the Hebrew Scriptures we have today.

The Septuagint (LXX)	This is a Greek translation of the Hebrew Old Testament begun around 250 BC and completed about one hundred years later. This Greek translation made it possible for non-Hebrew-speaking people in the ancient world to read God's Word. It was the translation used often in New Testament quotations of the Old Testament, and it became the version of choice for the early church fathers. "Septuagint," often abbreviated by the Roman numeral LXX (70), refers to the story that seventy translators worked on the initial translation project in Egypt.
Dead Sea Scrolls	The Dead Sea Scrolls contain no New Testament texts. These are a collection of writings discovered since 1948 in caves of the Qumran region near the Dead Sea in Israel. Most scholars believe they were composed or copied between 200 BC and AD 100. They contain important Hebrew manuscripts of Old Testament books and informative historical documents produced by the Qumran community—a Jewish separatist sect that followed a strict ascetic code and expected the end of the world to come soon.
Early Church Fathers	These writings are by pastors and teachers who lived after the apostles and prophets. They acknowledged that their writings did not carry the same authority as the canonical books. These writings often defended, explained, or applied some aspect of the canonical books or the orthodox faith. The term *apostolic fathers* refers to the early church fathers who are believed to have lived closest to the time of the apostles. While most of the writings of the early church fathers present the central teachings of orthodox Christianity, several represent fringe elements that eventually led to the formation of heretical groups.
Nag Hammadi Library	These writings are mostly Gnostic pseudepigraphic writings forged between the second and fourth centuries that advance heretical views about God and Christ. The thirteen volumes of numerous writings were discovered in Nag Hammadi, Egypt, in 1945, and have been the subject of intense study ever since. However, prior to this time, historians were aware of such ancient Gnostic documents through the references and quotations of similar heretical writings mentioned in the works of the early church fathers.

JESUS FOCUS
The Center of Scripture and History

by Derrick G. Jeter

I am the Alpha and the Omega, the first and the last, the beginning and the end" (Revelation 22:13). With these staggering and exclusive words, Jesus declared that He is the start and finish of history—all of history, not just biblical history.

In spite of His strong declaration, some will argue, "It is easy to accept Jesus as the subject of Scripture, certainly of the New Testament, and probably of the Old Testament. But the claim that Jesus is the focal point of history is stretching it a bit far . . . isn't it?" Let's briefly explore His assertion.

Jesus Christ: The Subject of Scripture

Defining Jesus as the subject of Scripture doesn't mean you'll find His name in every verse. Rather the story of Christ is told throughout the whole Bible; He is reflected in every book, every chapter.

In tracing the centrality of Jesus throughout the Bible, it seems logical to begin at the beginning. So let's do that; let's begin at the chronological beginning, as recorded in John 1. John tells us the "Word" was in the beginning with God and was God, and that all of creation was made by the Word, who is the source of life and light (John 1:1–5). Who is this creative Word? Jesus! (John 1:14–18). So when we turn back and read Genesis 1:1, "In the beginning God created the heavens and the earth," we are reading of the creative act of Jesus. Now, before you point out the obvious, I know that Genesis 1:1 says, "God created," not "Jesus created." Notice that in John 1:1, "the Word" equals God. Therefore, God and Jesus are one. The Holy Spirit is also one with Jesus (Acts 16:6–7). The ten-cent theological term we're describing is the *Trinity*. You can read

...more about it in "This We Believe: Basic Doctrines for Biblical Discernment" on page 79. So when Genesis 1:1 describes God as the Creator, it also applies to Jesus (see also Colossians 1:16).

After sin entered the world (Genesis 3), the Lord cursed Satan, promising that One would be born from a woman and someday "crush [Satan's] head" (Genesis 3:15 NIV). This provided the first indication of God's plan to redeem His creation through the ignoble death, glorious resurrection, and righteous reign of His Son, Jesus.

In the Old Testament, God's plan of redemption paints Jesus in broad strokes. In the books of the Law, Genesis through Deuteronomy, Jesus is pictured as the righteous, sacrificial Lamb who frees His people from bondage and brings healing (Exodus 12; John 1:29). The Historical books, Joshua through Esther, paint Jesus as the promised King who would restore His people (2 Samuel 7:16; Luke 1:32). The books of Wisdom and Poetry, Job through Song of Solomon, sing of Jesus as the Mediator between God and man (Job 16:19; 1 Timothy 2:5), as the object of our highest praise (Psalm 148; Philippians 2:9–11), and as the source of wisdom (Proverbs 2:6; Colossians 2:2–3). The books of the Prophets, Isaiah through Malachi, anticipate the Anointed One, the Messiah, the "Wonderful Counselor, Mighty God, Eternal Father, [and] Prince of Peace" (Isaiah 9:6; see also Matthew 1:23).

The New Testament fills in the fine details of Jesus's portrait. The Gospels, Matthew through John, provide a biography of Jesus as the long-awaited Messiah, the Son of Man and Son of God, who died and rose again (Matthew 16:16; Mark 10:33–34). The Historical book of Acts chronicles the early history of Christ's church, revealing Jesus as the triumphant Redeemer and Sender of those who believe to the "remotest part[s] of the earth" (Acts 1:8). The letters of Doctrine, Romans through Jude, teach that Jesus is the source of salvation, by grace, through faith in His death and resurrection (Romans 5:1). And by the power of His indwelling Spirit, we can live a Christlike life (Galatians 5:16). Finally, the book of Prophecy, Revelation, looks heavenward in anticipation of Jesus's return to finish His work of redeeming creation and to begin His earthly reign as King of kings and Lord of lords (Revelation 19:16).

Simply put, what the Old Testament anticipates and the New Testament celebrates is Jesus—*the* subject of Scripture.

Jesus Christ: The Focal Point of History

Now that we've proven that designating Jesus as the subject of Scripture is not too much of a stretch, let's take this line of reasoning a bit further. Of all the great men and women who have ever lived, can we really point to Jesus and say, "He is the apex of history"?

Solomon observed that God has "set eternity in [the human] heart" (Ecclesiastes 3:11). From the very beginning, regardless of time and place, men and women have wrestled with eternal questions regarding the existence of God, why and how we are here, where evil comes from and what can be done about it, and whether there is life after death. Proposed answers to these issues abound, but no one individual or philosophy has provided *the* answer to these questions or embodied the answer perfectly—until Jesus. Only in Him are the questions of Creation, the Fall, redemption, and restoration satisfactorily answered.

Many, of course, reject this truth as scandalous. Like a stone tripping up the toe of humanity, Jesus has never been an easy figure to dismiss. During His own ministry on earth, the religious leaders of the day scratched their heads over Jesus's power and authority. Men and women since Jesus have pondered His life and teaching with great bewilderment. Name any great religious thinker, political leader, philosopher, or artist, and you'll soon discover the name of Jesus—more than Buddha, Muhammad, Socrates, or Plato—on their lips or written by their pens. All who came before Jesus puzzled over the eternal questions He answered. All who've come after Him have struggled with the reality of the truth He lived and taught. None, whether before or after, have profoundly influenced individual lives or changed the course of civilization like Jesus Christ.

Of course, we who believe the Bible should not be surprised that Jesus is the focal point of history. He said it Himself: "I am the Alpha and the Omega, the first and the last, the beginning and the end" (Revelation 22:13). None can rival Him.

> God highly exalted Him, and bestowed on Him the
> name which is above every name, so that at the name of
> Jesus every knee will bow, of those who are in heaven
> and on earth and under the earth, and that every tongue
> will confess that Jesus Christ is Lord, to the glory of God
> the Father. (Philippians 2:9–11)

FASCINATING FACTS

- The Bible contains sixty-six books, written by forty authors, covering a period of approximately sixteen hundred years.

- The word *Bible* comes from the Greek word *biblos*, meaning "book."

- The word *testament* means "covenant" or "agreement."

- Jesus quoted from twenty-two Old Testament books.

- The book of Hebrews quotes the Old Testament eighty-five times.

- Revelation quotes the Old Testament 245 times.

IN OTHER WORDS
Differences in Bible Translations

by John Adair

D uring my college years, I worked in a Christian bookstore that
sported an entire wall of Bibles for sale. Customers would often
need assistance in navigating the wide variety of choices. One woman
was especially memorable. She looked back and forth along the wall
for more than an hour, laboring over her decision. Through extensive
conversation, we decided the New King James Version (NKJV) would be
best for her. She bought the Bible, only to come back to the store an hour
later demanding a refund. Apparently, in reading Numbers 31:11, she
found what she considered to be an offensive word. Of course, the word
she found in the NKJV originally comes from the King James Version
(KJV), which was compiled in 1611.

My customer was frustrated because she didn't understand one basic
difference between Bible translations—the development of language.
Translations differ in other ways as well, such as the sources from which
they are derived or the specific method of translation. With so many of
them being produced, we need to think carefully about these differences
and their impact on the Bibles we read and study.

Method of Translation

Each version of the Bible has a particular way of converting the language from the original Greek, Hebrew, and Aramaic into English. These
approaches can be broken into three broad categories: formal equivalence, dynamic equivalence, and the paraphrase.

The New American Standard Bible (NASB) and the NKJV are great
examples of translations that aspire to *formal equivalence*. This type of
translation attempts to keep as much of the original form of the language

as possible, seeking to follow the original text word-for-word. Translations governed by a formal equivalence approach are strong on accuracy, though they can be less readable than others.

Dynamic equivalence focuses primarily on readability and communicating the meaning of the text in the English language rather than preserving the outward forms of the original languages. The New International Version (NIV) and the more recent New Living Translation (NLT) are a couple of popular examples that fall into this category. These translations render the meaning of the passage by following the original manuscript phrase-for-phrase or thought-for-thought as opposed to word-for-word.

One issue that's come up regarding dynamic equivalence in recent years is the use of gender-neutral language. Today's New International Version (TNIV) is the best-known translation to attempt this linguistic change. Rather than going to the extremes of some by removing all masculine or feminine language from the Bible, the TNIV attempts to remove only the generic masculine language that would properly be directed at both men and women. (For an example, compare the NASB and the TNIV translations of Matthew 23:5, where the Greek term *anthropois* clearly has both men and women in view. The NASB translates the word as "men," and the TNIV translates it as "people.") However, the TNIV is far from an unqualified success, as quite a large number of respected Christian leaders feel it goes too far in its removal of such language.

The third approach to translation is the *paraphrase*, adopted by highly readable versions like The Living Bible (LB) and Eugene Peterson's The Message (MSG). Not technically translations, these versions communicate the ideas of the text, while stretching beyond many of the particulars of language and grammar. It's helpful to think of paraphrases as a kind of running commentary, expanding words and phrases from the original as needed to communicate the biblical meaning to the modern reader.

Translation Source

An accurate translation demands working with manuscripts in the original language. While we don't possess the original manuscripts themselves, we do have reliable ancient copies. The Bible stands alone among ancient texts with the sheer breadth of documentary evidence that has come down to us. As centuries go by, we discover more and more manuscripts, in some cases copied earlier than anything we previously possessed. Therefore, those who created an older translation like the KJV had access to fewer pieces of manuscript evidence than, say, those who created the NASB. With such a wide variety of older sources to use these days, there is a running dialogue among scholars about which sources are most accurate. Some believe the earliest sources should be favored. The majority of modern translations tend to follow this pattern. Others argue for following the greatest number of sources that support a particular reading, no matter how late they were copied. An older version like the KJV follows this translation pattern.

Development of Language

Not surprisingly, the meaning of words changes over time. New ideas are associated with existing words. Some words fall out of use. Because language varies, new translations of the Bible can be helpful in communicating the truths of this ancient Book. Remember, no matter the version we read in English, it's already gone through some language development in the process of translation. But don't worry; conscientious, reliable translators always ground their work in the original languages.

A variety of English translations can also be helpful, depending on the context. Something like the NASB or the NKJV might serve best for study, while the NIV or the MSG make for a more pleasurable reading experience. Finding the right Bible for you need not be a difficult task, because every translation has unique strengths in bringing the Word of God into English.

So when it's time for a new Bible and you head down to the local bookstore, you might very well encounter a wall of Bibles like my customer did. Having a sense of the differences between versions and outlining some personal preferences in advance should help streamline the process of selection. Whichever version you choose, the most important choice you'll make is the one to spend time reading it.

BIBLE TRANSLATIONS

Version	Type of Translation	Year Published	Readability
King James Version (KJV)	Formal Equivalence	1611	Difficult to read due to archaic language; important as literature due to extensive use since its publication.
New American Standard Bible (NASB)	Formal Equivalence	1971	Word-for-word translation; good for study; accurate but a bit wooden.
New International Version (NIV)	Dynamic Equivalence	1978	The most popular translation; good for casual reading.
New King James Version (NKJV)	Formal Equivalence	1979	Preserves the reverent feel of the KJV while updating its language.
The New Century Version (NCV)	Dynamic Equivalence	1986	Simple language; good for elementary-school-age children.
The New Revised Standard Version (NRSV)	Formal Equivalence	1990	Solid study Bible; language a bit removed from contemporary usage.
New Living Translation (NLT)	Dynamic Equivalence	1996	Presents the Bible in common, everyday speech.
The New English Translation (NET)	Dynamic/ Formal Equivalence	1997	Better flow than most formal translations; stronger accuracy than most dynamic translations; extensive notes for study.
The Holy Bible: English Standard Version (ESV)	Formal Equivalence	2001	Great for study; good use of language, though occasionally stilted.
The Message (MSG)	Paraphrase	2000	Easy to read; conversational; good for casual reading.
Today's New International Version (TNIV)	Dynamic Equivalence	2005	Based on NIV; easy to read with its contemporary language; gender neutral (see discussion above).

GOING PLACES
Understanding Biblical Geography

by Wayne Stiles

M any places in the land of the Bible have familiar names: the Sea of Galilee, Jerusalem, Jericho, and the Mount of Olives. Yet without an understanding of where each name fits in relation to another, the places can seem disheveled in our minds—like spilled puzzle pieces without the top of the box for perspective.

I shared this frustration. For the vast majority of my Christian life, the benefits of understanding the land of the Bible remained hidden like artifacts in the sand. I possessed knowledge of the places' names, sure, but they played no role in my study of the Bible except to distract and confuse me. Because I couldn't appreciate a site's contribution to the biblical narrative, I dismissed the unfamiliar as irrelevant or, at the very least, of minor importance.

But as I began to study the simple geography of the Bible . . . it all changed. I discovered an integral part of Bible study that I had missed all my life. Like seeing the whole puzzle put together, I was now able to see the individual sites in light of the whole. My memory of biblical events was strengthened by associating the events with their geographical locations. What I had dismissed earlier as irrelevant I began to recognize as an *essential* part of God's dealings with His people.

Knowing something of the Bible's geography helps us in a number of important ways as we approach God's Word.

Biblical Geography: Interpreting the Bible's Meaning

Before we come to Scripture and ask, "What does this passage mean to me?" we must understand what it means in context, including what it meant to the original readers. Context means more than the words before

27

and after a passage. It also includes geography—the stage and setting of the biblical drama.

For example, King Asa of Jerusalem once trusted the Lord in a battle to the south and defeated an army a million strong. But when the northern king Baasha fortified Ramah—which sat only five miles north of Jerusalem—Asa decided to take the silver and gold from the treasuries of the temple (that he had dedicated to God!) and solicit help from the pagan king of Aram. Why would Asa, who earlier had the faith to gain victory over a million men, suddenly panic and look to his own devices for help? Because God took from Asa something he trusted in more than God—a parcel of land. Asa could not fathom what he would do without the strategic plateau surrounding Ramah. So he scrambled to get it back at all costs (2 Chronicles 14; 16). As with Asa, we often have no problem trusting God when we feel secure. But what do we do when God says to give Him our most precious possessions? We learn from Asa that God may remove what we depend on the most so that we will learn to trust in Him alone. The geography of the passage makes this clear.

Biblical Geography: Validating the Bible's Claims

Nineteenth-century archaeologist William Ramsay began his career with the general assumption that the book of Acts contained careless, geographical errors written by someone ignorant of Asia Minor. However, after Ramsay traveled throughout Asia Minor (modern-day Turkey), he altered his position. He found the geography presented in Acts accurate in every detail—and he believed the message of the book.

Jesus said, "If I told you earthly things and you do not believe, how will you believe if I tell you heavenly things?" (John 3:12). The truth we see in earthly, physical things gives credence to those heavenly untouchables God tells us about. When the Bible talks about the Kidron Valley lying east of Jerusalem, or Capernaum beside the Sea of Galilee, these statements are facts we can verify today. Studying biblical geography provides us with a deeper appreciation of God as the Lord of world history and also of seemingly minor details, which brings extreme comfort to our lives . . . and increased confidence in God's Word.

Biblical Geography: Applying the Bible's Truths

At the beginning of His ministry, Jesus moved His base of operations from the sleepy town of Nazareth to the bustling city of Capernaum by the Sea of Galilee to fulfill "what was spoken through Isaiah the prophet" (Matthew 4:14). While several cities along the shore could have fulfilled this prophecy, it seems Jesus's selection of Capernaum had more deliberate purposes. A thriving fishing village, Capernaum straddled the international highway that stretched from Syria to Egypt. By choosing Capernaum, Jesus selected a city that enjoyed a constant flow of people who could carry His message to many places. And that's just what happened (4:24–25).

When we understand the geographical awareness of Jesus, we come to understand a strategy that we, too, should apply. In our lives and ministries, we must not merely exist but also live strategically. In what location or vocation can we best serve the Lord? What represents the best use of our time for God's glory? Sometimes, these answers require a major move—as was the case with Jesus. But sometimes, we simply need to change our thinking and ask ourselves, *Is the kingdom of God really the goal of my life?*

* * *

I have found it true again and again; the better I understand the land of the Bible, the better I understand the Bible itself. A recent survey administered during the course of doctoral research revealed some astounding statistics. For 97 percent of those who took the survey, taking a class on biblical geography improved their understanding of the Bible. And an astounding 99 percent of those who have traveled to Israel agreed that experiencing the Holy Land had strengthened their spiritual life.[2]

Don't misunderstand these results. Studying biblical geography won't provide some long-lost secret to a higher spiritual life. And traveling to Israel won't gain you more favor with God. But the study of the land of the Bible provides a deeper, clearer, and more vibrant understanding of the truth that God has *already* revealed. And that truth—God's Word— changes lives.

The Bible bursts with geographical references on almost every page, but they never yielded their fruit to me as a casual observer. But when I peered into the text for its details and opened an atlas . . . my, what treasures awaited![3]

MAPS

JERUSALEM

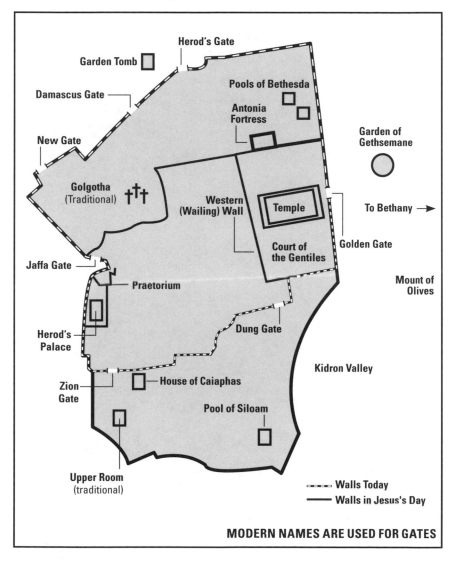

Herod's Gate

Garden Tomb

Pools of Bethesda

Damascus Gate

Antonia Fortress

Garden of Gethsemane

New Gate

Golgotha (Traditional) ✝✝✝

Western (Wailing) Wall

Temple

To Bethany →

Court of the Gentiles

Golden Gate

Jaffa Gate

Praetorium

Mount of Olives

Herod's Palace

Dung Gate

Kidron Valley

Zion Gate

House of Caiaphas

Pool of Siloam

Upper Room (traditional)

╍╍╍ Walls Today

▬▬ Walls in Jesus's Day

MODERN NAMES ARE USED FOR GATES

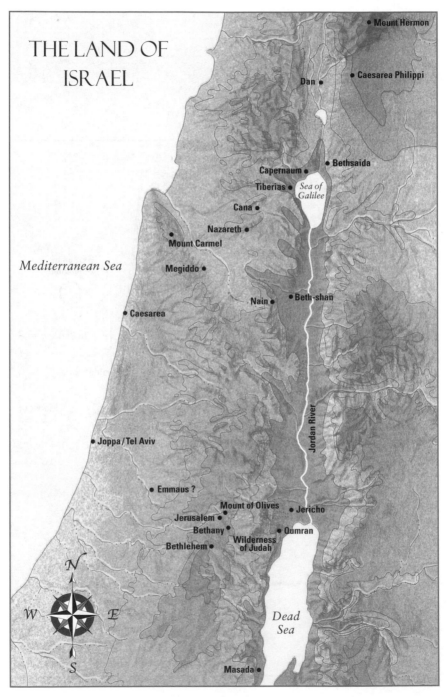

THE LAND OF
ISRAEL

Mount Hermon

Caesarea Philippi

Dan

Bethsaida

Capernaum

Tiberias

Sea of
Galilee

Cana

Nazareth

Mount Carmel

Mediterranean Sea

Megiddo

Nain

Beth-shan

Caesarea

Jordan River

Joppa / Tel Aviv

Emmaus ?

Mount of Olives

Jericho

Jerusalem

Bethany

Qumran

Bethlehem

Wilderness
of Judah

Dead
Sea

Masada

N

W   E

S

HISTORY
AND THE Bible

THE NOISY SILENT YEARS
The Times between the Testaments

by Michael J. Svigel

In two of Daniel's mystifying visions, he saw the future of his people and of the land of Israel unfold from the time of the Babylonian Empire to the coming of the Messiah (Daniel 2; 7). These visions primarily focused on the violently shifting political landscape during the nearly four hundred years of prophetic "silence" from the writing of the last book of the Old Testament, Malachi, around 430 BC, to the preaching of John the Baptist around AD 26.

What transpired during these centuries of silence set the stage for the coming of the Messiah and the preaching of the gospel of salvation to the ends of the earth. These "silent centuries" can be divided into four distinct periods.

The Persian Period (450–330 BC)

For about one hundred years after Nehemiah's time, the Persian Empire controlled Judea. During that time, the Jews were allowed to carry on their religious observances without foreign interference. The high priests and governors ruled over Judea; the temple of Solomon, which had been destroyed by the Babylonians, was replaced by a smaller temple in Jerusalem; and the people of Israel continued to recover from the devastation they had previously endured at the hands of the Babylonians (2 Kings 24; 25; 2 Chronicles 36).

The Hellenistic Period (330–166 BC)

In 333 BC, the Persian armies stationed in Macedonia were defeated by Alexander the Great. He was convinced that Hellenism—the Greek culture and language—was the one force that could unify the world. Alexander permitted the Jews to continue observing their laws, even ɡ them exemption from tribute or tax during their Sabbath —every seventh year. The Greek conquest prepared the way for ɹranslation of the Old Testament into Greek around 250 BC, allowing ɹ Jewish Scriptures to be read by Greek-speaking Gentiles. During this ρeriod, too, the Pharisees arose as a popular legalistic religious sect dedicated to the rigorous observance of the Mosaic Law in every aspect of life, marking the birth of what eventually became Rabbinical Judaism.

The Hasmonean Period (166–63 BC)

After the death of Alexander the Great, his vast empire was divided among his four generals. Judea first fell under the rule of the Ptolemies, who had been tolerant of the Jews and their religious practices. However, when the Seleucid rulers conquered Judea, they were determined to force the Greek language, culture, and even religion upon the proud and protective Jews. Copies of the Scriptures were destroyed, and laws were enforced with extreme cruelty. The mad ruler, Antiochus Epiphanes, outlawed circumcision, put an end to temple sacrifices, and even offered swine on the altar, desecrating the temple. Led by Judas Maccabeus, the oppressed Jews revolted, and for a short period of time Judea was liberated from its oppressors.

The Roman Period (63 BC–New Testament era)

In the year 63 BC, the Roman general Pompey captured Jerusalem, and the provinces of Judea became subject to the iron-fisted rule of Rome. The local government was entrusted part of the time to princes and the rest of the time to procurators, or governors, who were appointed by the emperors. Herod Antipas was appointed by Rome to act as "king" over Judea, a position he held at the time of Christ's ministry, while Pontius Pilate served as the Roman procurator. During this period, the Romans built a massive system of roads and cities, making commerce, transportation, and communication faster and more reliable than ever.

God's Work Never Ceases

Galatians 4:4 says, "When the fullness of the time came, God sent His Son." In God's sovereign plan and according to His perfect timing, Jesus was born. As we reflect on the centuries of "silence" between the Testaments, we see that God was active, setting the stage for the coming of Christ and the preaching of the gospel. Because of the peace of the Persians, the Jews returned to the land of Judea, rebuilt their cities and temple, and grew in size and strength. Because of the Greeks, the world was united by a common language into which God's Word could be translated and by which a universal message of salvation could be preached. Because of the persecution by the Seleucids and the oppression by the Romans, Jews living in bondage began to look with hope at the prophecies of a coming Messiah who would fulfill the promises of salvation and freedom. And also through Roman rule, roads were built to connect all of the major centers of civilization, allowing for rapid travel, communication, and the spread of the good news from Jerusalem as far as Spain within just a few decades.

While most of our Bibles transition from Malachi to Matthew with the turn of just a few pages, we should not forget the period of long, silent centuries during which God was still working out His plan.

BIBLICAL AREAS AND NATIONS*

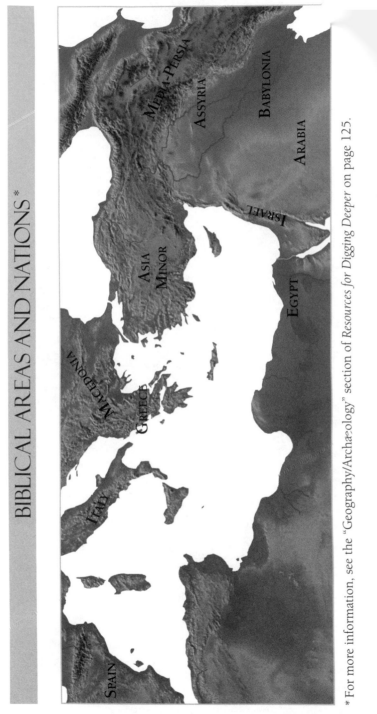

* For more information, see the "Geography/Archæology" section of *Resources for Digging Deeper* on page 125.

NEW TESTAMENT SECTS AND PARTIES

Sect or Party	Beliefs
Pharisees	The Pharisees were the orthodox religious sect of the Jews, known for their strict adherence to the written Law and to Jewish traditions. They believed in life after death, looked forward to the resurrection of the dead, and believed that God's sovereignty and human free will were compatible. Known for zealously maintaining a lifestyle of adherence to the Law even outside the shadow of the temple, the Pharisaic tradition, which had come into existence around 200 BC, eventually became the basis for Rabbinical Orthodox Judaism. Jesus did not condemn the Pharisees' theology or zeal but their legalism and hypocrisy. See Matthew 23:23; Acts 23:6–8.
Scribes	These Jews, often closely associated with Pharisees (Matthew 23:13), studied, interpreted, and taught the Law like Ezra in the Old Testament (Ezra 7:10). They were also called "lawyers" or "teachers of the Law" (Matthew 22:35; Acts 5:34). Because of their expertise in Jewish Law, scribes often served as judges on legal matters.
Sadducees	The Sadducees were a sect of the Jews who had political power—especially over the temple administration—but had little popular influence. They denied a spiritual afterlife, a future resurrection, and a coming judgment. They also rejected the traditional interpretations of the Law developed by the rabbis and Pharisees and advocated freedom of the human will. Because their power was so closely related to the temple, the Sadducees disappeared as a Jewish sect after the destruction of the temple in AD 70.
Essenes	The Essenes were a strict separatist party of Jews who believed they were God's remnant. They condemned the corrupt temple priesthood and the "compromising" lifestyle of most Jews, including the Pharisees. They often withdrew into the wilderness to live in small communities and await the coming of the end, when all things would be restored to the true remnant of Israel. The community of people who copied and preserved the Dead Sea Scrolls in Qumran were likely Essenes.

Sect or Party	Beliefs
Priests	The Israelites who formed the tribe of Levi were responsible for worship in the temple. Though many of the rulers of the temple were Sadducees, many priests themselves were not. The function of the priesthood ended with the destruction of the temple in AD 70, and the role of teaching the Law was taken over by the Pharisaic rabbis.
Zealots	These nationalist Jews sought to drive out the Romans and reestablish Israel as an independent and sovereign kingdom. Zealots often engaged in assassination and terrorist-like activities directed at both Romans and influential Jews who cooperated with the Romans.
Gnostics	Gnostics believed a mystical mixture of Greek philosophy, Eastern religion, mythology, and Christianity. They sought salvation only for the spiritual part of humans through *gnosis*— special knowledge. Though this Christian heresy did not develop until the second century, traces of a pre-Gnostic heresy seem to have troubled the church in Colossae (Colossians 2:2–3) and perhaps other churches (1 Timothy 6:20).
Docetists	By the end of the first century, a group of heretics denied the real, physical, fleshly humanity of Christ, claiming that the Lord was either a purely immaterial spirit—like an angel—or a spiritual being (Christ) who temporarily possessed a physical human (Jesus). Thus, the heavenly Son of God only "appeared" (Greek *dokeo*) to be human. The Gospel of John and the book of 1 John both address this false teaching by emphasizing the fleshly reality of the incarnation (John 1:14; 1 John 1:1–3).

BIBLE HISTORY TIMELINE

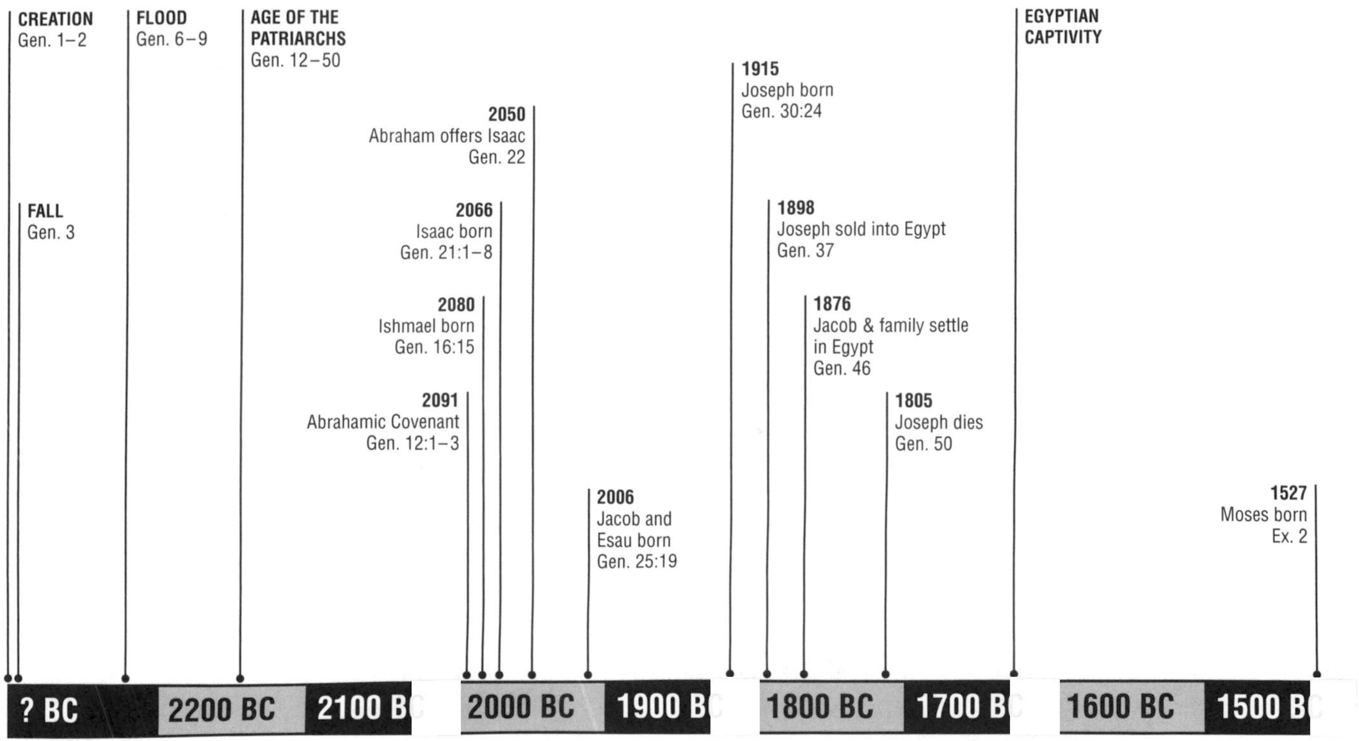

CREATION Gen. 1–2	FLOOD Gen. 6–9	AGE OF THE PATRIARCHS Gen. 12–50						EGYPTIAN CAPTIVITY

FALL
Gen. 3

2050
Abraham offers Isaac
Gen. 22

2066
Isaac born
Gen. 21:1–8

2080
Ishmael born
Gen. 16:15

2091
Abrahamic Covenant
Gen. 12:1–3

2006
Jacob and
Esau born
Gen. 25:19

1915
Joseph born
Gen. 30:24

1898
Joseph sold into Egypt
Gen. 37

1876
Jacob & family settle
in Egypt
Gen. 46

1805
Joseph dies
Gen. 50

1527
Moses born
Ex. 2

? BC	2200 BC	2100 BC	2000 BC	1900 BC	1800 BC	1700 BC	1600 BC	1500 BC

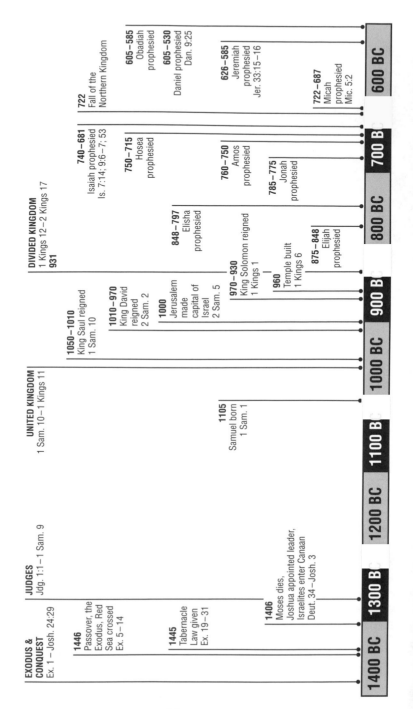

BIBLE HISTORY TIMELINE, CONT.

EXODUS & CONQUEST
Ex. 1 – Josh. 24:29

JUDGES
Jdg. 1:1 – 1 Sam. 9

UNITED KINGDOM
1 Sam. 10 – 1 Kings 11

DIVIDED KINGDOM
1 Kings 12 – 2 Kings 17
931

1446
Passover, the Exodus, Red Sea crossed
Ex. 5 – 14

1445
Tabernacle Law given
Ex. 19 – 31

1406
Moses dies, Joshua appointed leader, Israelites enter Canaan
Deut. 34 – Josh. 3

1105
Samuel born
1 Sam. 1

1050 – 1010
King Saul reigned
1 Sam. 10

1010 – 970
King David reigned
2 Sam. 2

1000
Jerusalem made capital of Israel
2 Sam. 5

970 – 930
King Solomon reigned
1 Kings 1

960
Temple built
1 Kings 6

875 – 848
Elijah prophesied

848 – 797
Elisha prophesied

740 – 681
Isaiah prophesied
Is. 7:14; 9:6 – 7; 53

750 – 715
Hosea prophesied

760 – 750
Amos prophesied

785 – 775
Jonah prophesied

722
Fall of the Northern Kingdom

605 – 585
Obadiah prophesied

605 – 530
Daniel prophesied
Dan. 9:25

626 – 585
Jeremiah prophesied
Jer. 33:15 – 16

722 – 687
Micah prophesied
Mic. 5:2

1400 BC   1300 BC   1200 BC   1100 BC   1000 BC   900 BC   800 BC   700 BC   600 BC

44

BIBLE HISTORY TIMELINE, CONT.

FALL OF JERUSALEM
586

EXILE
Daniel

RESTORATION
Ezra–Esther

593–571
Ezekiel prophesied
Ezek. 37:24–25

538
Temple Rebuilt
First group returns with Zerubbabel

520–480
Zechariah prophesied
Zech. 9:9

440–430
Malachi prophesied
Mal. 3:1

458
Second group returns with Ezra

432
Third group returns with Nehemiah

BETWEEN THE TESTAMENTS

356–323
Alexander the Great reigned
Rise of Greek Empire

250
Septuagint translated

175–164
Antiochus IV Epiphanes reigned

167
Maccabean Revolt

44
Julius Caesar assassinated

27 BC–AD 14
Augustus Caesar reigned
Rise of Roman Empire

37–4
Herod the Great reigned

CHRIST'S EARLY LIFE
Matt. 1-2; Luke 1-2

5/4
Christ born

4
Herod the Great dies

8/9
Christ in the temple (age 12)

500 BC · 400 BC · 300 BC · 200 BC · 100 BC · BC · AD · AD 10

BIBLE HISTORY TIMELINE, CONT.

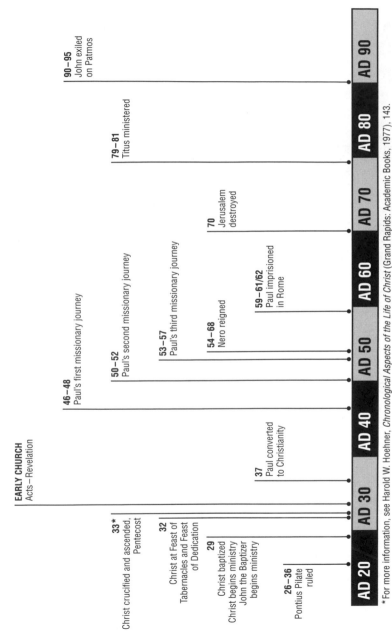

EARLY CHURCH
Acts – Revelation

AD 20   **AD 30**   **AD 40**   **AD 50**   **AD 60**   **AD 70**   **AD 80**   **AD 90**

26–36
Pontius Pilate ruled

29
Christ baptized
Christ begins ministry
John the Baptizer begins ministry

32
Christ at Feast of Tabernacles and Feast of Dedication

33*
Christ crucified and ascended, Pentecost

37
Paul converted to Christianity

46–48
Paul's first missionary journey

50–52
Paul's second missionary journey

53–57
Paul's third missionary journey

54–68
Nero reigned

59–61/62
Paul imprisioned in Rome

70
Jerusalem destroyed

79–81
Titus ministered

90–95
John exiled on Patmos

* For more information, see Harold W. Hoehner, *Chronological Aspects of the Life of Christ* (Grand Rapids: Academic Books, 1977), 143.

FATHERS AND REFORMERS
Carrying on the Biblical Tradition

by Michael J. Svigel

With martyrdom looming before him, the apostle Paul charged Timothy with the following task: "The things which you have heard from me in the presence of many witnesses, entrust these to faithful men who will be able to teach others also" (2 Timothy 2:2).

Did Timothy succeed, or did he drop the ball? Did the flame of the Spirit continue to burn brightly in the first centuries following the apostles, or was the light extinguished by false prophets, politics, and persecution?

Fathers of the Faith

Christians as well as skeptics are often surprised to learn that we don't have to scratch our heads and wonder what happened to the church after the New Testament era. Though few Christians have read them, we have access to the writings of second- and third-generation believers, known as the apostolic fathers and apologists. Without God working through the radical faith of these early Christians, the New Testament writings would have been lost like ashes in the wind and the gospel would have suffocated under a smothering heap of heresy.

Remember Clement, who was mentioned in Philippians 4:3? He became pastor of the church in Rome and wrote a long letter to the church at Corinth in the AD 90s. Polycarp, the pastor of Smyrna, was ordained by the apostle John himself. And Ignatius, pastor of Antioch until AD 110, likely knew the last living apostles. After these men, we have writings from the next generation of leaders, including Justin, a famous teacher in Rome around AD 150, and Irenaeus, the pastor of Lyons around AD 180—both of whom had probably known Polycarp, the protégé of John. So we can explore for ourselves the writings of the

.iul men (Clement, Ignatius, and Polycarp) who were able to teach
ıers (Justin and Irenaeus). Paul's solemn charge to Timothy was indeed
ılfilled (2 Timothy 2:2).

These early heroes of the faith kept the torchlight of the gospel
burning through some of the most difficult periods of persecution and
false teaching the church has ever known, all of them fueling the flames
with their own heroic martyrdoms. Against dangerous heresies they
stood their ground and suffered severely, preserving Scripture and the
fundamentals of the faith against formidable foes. Clement of Rome
was martyred during the great persecution of Domitian in AD 96. The
Romans threw Ignatius of Antioch to the wild beasts around AD 110.
Polycarp suffered the pyre in Smyrna around AD 155. Justin was
beheaded in Rome after waging a war of words with powerful philosophers in that city.

In stark contrast, very few heretics bothered to seal their deceitful
doctrines with martyrdom. In fact, these false teachers often mocked true
Christians for going to such extremes. "After all," they reasoned, "Jesus
didn't have a real body and didn't really suffer and die as you believe, so
why should we?" They altered their theology to fit their philosophy and
experience. And they reinterpreted the Bible to support their agendas.

The Medieval Decline

In the fourth and fifth centuries, as the Roman Empire first legalized
Christianity and then embraced it, the pastors and teachers of the church
grew in power and prestige. A few bright lights shone amidst the
encroaching darkness, however. Augustine of Hippo contended against
the heretic Pelagius, who taught that humans could reform themselves
by their own strength and thus merit God's grace and mercy. Augustine
argued that our salvation and any good thing we believe or do is a result
of God's sovereign grace and mercy, not of our human ability and effort.
Yet, after Augustine, the Roman Catholic Church gradually moved away
from the biblical gospel of salvation by grace through faith apart from
works, teaching instead a salvation based on earning God's grace by par-
ticipation in the sacraments of the church.

Later in the Middle Ages, with the rise of Christian philosophers and scholars, the basic truths of Scripture were interpreted in the light of philosophical systems, church councils, creeds, laws, and an ever-enlarging body of traditions that could not be substantiated either by Scripture or by the most ancient traditions of the church. Eventually the decrees of the pope became the final standard of religious authority, and the pope's interpretation of the Bible was regarded by Roman Catholics as infallible.

In the midst of the Middle Ages, spiritual ignorance shrouded the world, and corruption darkened the established church. John Wycliffe (1320–1384) lit the flame of truth when he protested that the Scriptures, only available to the clergy and set in the dead language of Latin, were not accessible to the people. In 1382 he finished translating the Latin Vulgate into English . . . paying for it with persecution from the Catholic Church.

Though John Huss (1370–1415) knew that the church had stripped Wycliffe of his position at Oxford, forbade him to preach, and burned his exhumed body after his death, Huss continued to expose hypocrisy in the church and elevate the truth of Scripture. Huss's words were temporarily silenced when he was covered in pitch and oil and set on fire . . . but his message was reignited a century later by the voice of Martin Luther.

Sparking the Reformation

As a monk bound by the works-based religion he had inherited from the medieval Catholic Church, Luther struggled to comprehend how a sinful man could stand under the scrutiny of a holy and exacting God. As a scholar, he began reading the forgotten teachings of Augustine, then studying the Bible for himself in the original languages. In his studies he discovered the words that set him free: "But the righteous man shall live by faith" (Romans 1:17). Once he understood that righteousness is a gift that comes by faith in Christ alone—not by works—he heralded the message of justification by faith alone and condemned the church for its unscriptural teachings that had abandoned not only the faith of the ancient fathers but the very words of the Bible itself!

Luther also protested the hypocrisy and moral debauchery of the clergy, the biblical illiteracy of both the congregation and the priests, and the unabashed materialism among church leaders. Many priests had fallen into lust and licentious living; common people had little access to the Bible because it was kept locked away; and church leaders charged money for numerous rites and rituals, such as baptisms, weddings, and hearing confessions. In fact, the practice of selling indulgences—letters from the pope conferring spiritual merit that would release the buyers or their dead loved ones from purgatorial suffering—epitomized the corruption of the religious authorities.

Martin Luther, who understood that the only way to receive forgiveness of sin was by accepting it as a free gift from God, refused to stand by and watch religious charlatans extort money from the people with false doctrines found nowhere in the Bible. So at noon on October 31, 1517, Luther nailed his Ninety-five Theses to the door of Castle Church in Wittenberg, Germany, unaware of the great influence it would have on other European Reformers, such as Ulrich Zwingli and John Calvin, or on future generations. In carrying out such fervent, faith-based beliefs, the Reformers started a blaze that would burn throughout Europe and radically change Christian practices and beliefs for centuries to come.

However, as they had responded to Wycliffe and Huss before, the Roman Catholic Church struck back. At the famous trial in the city of Worms, Luther was called upon to renounce his "heretical" theology: "Do you recant, or do you not?"

With the fates of Wycliffe and Huss hanging over his own head, Luther announced:

> Unless I am overcome by the testimonies of Scripture
> or by clear reasoning—for I believe neither the pope nor
> the councils alone, because it is clear as day that they
> have often erred and contradicted themselves—
> I am overcome by the Holy Scriptures I have quoted.

My conscience is held captive by God's Word. I cannot and will not recant anything, because it is unsafe and dangerous to go against the conscience. Here I stand. I cannot do otherwise. God help me! Amen.[4]

After defying both pope and emperor based on the Word of God, Luther came under the protection of German nobles. During his long stay at Wartburg Castle, where he was placed for safekeeping after refusing to recant his beliefs, Luther translated the Bible into German. His translation of the New Testament, printed in 1522, represented a monumental step in getting Scripture to the people of Germany. As a result, Luther's countrymen had the opportunity to gain greater biblical knowledge and come to a saving faith in Jesus Christ.

Carrying on the Biblical Tradition

Today, Bible-believing Christians stand on the shoulders of those faithful saints who have gone before. We must remember the ancient church fathers who defended the gospel and the Bible from pagans . . . and revive the spirit of the great Reformers who rediscovered the clear gospel of grace through faith and reestablished Scripture as the supreme authority over novel traditions and the false teachings of men.

And, like the great Fathers and Reformers of centuries past, each of us has a decision to make: we can either snuff out the light of God's Word with passivity and fear or fan the flame by passing it on to future generations. The words of Paul to Timothy could have been written to each of us today: "The things which you have heard from me in the presence of many witnesses, entrust these to faithful men who will be able to teach others also" (2 Timothy 2:2).

WISE WORDS FROM THE FATHERS AND REFORMERS

You have searched the Scriptures, which are true, which were given by the Holy Spirit; you know that nothing unrighteous or counterfeit is written in them.[5]

—Clement of Rome (circa AD 95)

The entire Scriptures, the prophets, and the Gospels, can be clearly, unambiguously, and harmoniously understood by all, although all do not believe them.[6]

—Irenaeus of Lyons (circa AD 185)

These [books of the Bible] are fountains of salvation, that they who thirst may be satisfied with the living words they contain. In these alone is proclaimed the doctrine of godliness. Let no man add to these, neither let him take ought from these.[7]

—Athanasius of Alexandria (AD 367)

I simply taught, preached, and wrote God's Word; otherwise I did nothing. And while I slept . . . the Word so greatly weakened the papacy that no prince or emperor ever inflicted such losses upon it. I did nothing; the Word did everything.[8]

—Martin Luther (AD 1522)

Scripture bears upon the face of it as clear evidence of its truth, as white and black do of their colour, sweet and bitter of their taste.[9]

—John Calvin (AD 1559)

CHURCH HISTORY TIMELINE

ERA OF THE APOSTOLIC FATHERS
100–150
Earliest leaders after the apostles

ERA OF THE APOLOGISTS
125–300
Defended Christianity against critics and enemies

110–165
Justin Martyr
Defended Christianity as the "true philosophy" from the Old Testament prophets

120–200
Irenaeus of Lyons
Wrote against heresies; was first to explicitly acknowledge only four Gospels

ERA OF THE THEOLOGIANS
300–500
Formulated and defined the faith using technical expressions

182–251
Origen of Alexandria
Infamous for speculative theology and allegorical interpretations

300–373
Athanasius of Alexandria
Affirmed the entire New Testament Canon

318
Edict of Milan
Ended persecution of Christians

325
Council of Nicaea
Affirmed full deity of the Son

354–428
Augustine of Hippo
Defended doctrine of God's unmerited grace in salvation

381
Council of Constantinople
Affirmed doctrine of the Trinity

397
Council of Carthage
Confirmed the New Testament Canon

405
Jerome completes the Latin Vulgate

451
Council of Chalcedon
Affirmed Christ's two natures in one Person

EARLY MIDDLE AGES
500–1050
Increase in the political influence of the Eastern and Western Catholic churches

540–605
Gregory the Great
Regarded by Protestants as the first pope

| AD 100 | AD 200 | AD 300 | AD 400 | AD 500 |

55

CHURCH HISTORY TIMELINE, CONT.

HIGH MIDDLE AGES
1050–1300
Increase of monasticism, mysticism, scholasticism, and ecclesiastical power

1054
Great Schism between Eastern and Western Catholic churches over authority of the pope to change the Creed of Constantinople

1090–1153
Bernard of Clairvaux
Led the second great monastic reform and founded Cistercian order of monks

1095–1099
First Crusade
Began centuries of Christian warfare with Islam and Byzantium

ERA OF SCHOLASTICISM
1000–1500
Explored and systematized theology and philosophy, founded universities

1033–1109
Anselm of Canterbury
Articulated the doctrine of Christ's substitutionary atonement

787
Council of Nicaea II
Confirmed veneration of icons in worship

909–926
Monastery at Cluny became a center of reform in the church

675–749
John of Damascus
Defended use of images (icons) in worship

622
Founding of Islam

| AD 600 | AD 700 | AD 800 | AD 900 | AD 1000 |

CHURCH HISTORY TIMELINE, CONT.

RENAISSANCE PERIOD
1300–1500
Characterized by a rebirth of art, architecture, and learning, and a rediscovery of classical Greek and Latin literature, including the Greek New Testament

LATE MIDDLE AGES
1300–1500
Rise of papal power and corruption as well as early attempts at reforming the Catholic Church

AGE OF REFORM
1450–1600
Life and work of European Reformers and founding of the Protestant denominations

EARLY MODERN PERIOD
1500–1750
Optimistic confidence in human reason over divine revelation to solve problems of humanity; rise of rationalism, empiricism, and the scientific method

1225–1274
Thomas Aquinas
Medieval Catholicism's "greatest theologian"; synthesized theology and philosophy, revelation and reason; his writings were placed alongside Scripture as the theological authority of Roman Catholicism

1180–1226
Francis of Assisi
Took a vow of poverty and founded the Franciscan order of monks

1330–1384
John Wycliffe
Persecuted for translating the Bible into English and criticizing Roman Catholic corruption

1372–1415
John Huss
Burned at the stake for challenging Roman Catholic theology

1455
Gutenberg Bible printed

1483–1546
Martin Luther
Started the Protestant Reformation in Germany and translated the Bible into German

1509–1564
John Calvin
Led the Swiss Reformation and wrote the first systematic theology of the Reformed faith

1545–1564
Council of Trent
Roman Catholic counter-Reformation, adding the Apocrypha to the canon of Scripture, condemning Protestants, and affirming the authority of the pope

| AD 1100 | AD 1200 | AD 1300 | AD 1400 | AD 1500 |

LATE MODERN PERIOD
1750–1900
The "Enlightenment," characterized by destructive criticism of Scripture and rise of liberal theologies that sought to redefine Christianity according to modern science and philosophy

POSTMODERN PERIOD
1920–Present
Reacted against optimism of modern period, including confidence in human reason and the attainment of certainty in truth

1925–1950
Rise of evangelicalism, emphasizing orthodox theology, personal conversion, and the inerrancy of Scripture

1886–1968
Karl Barth
Reacted against liberal theology, but denied inerrancy of Scripture, ushering in neo-orthodox and neo-liberal theologies

1875–1925
The modernist-fundamentalist controversy, division of Protestant denominations into liberal and conservative churches

1703–1758
Jonathan Edwards
American theologian emphasized God's sovereignty and holiness

1611
King James Bible translated

| AD 1600 | AD 1700 | AD 1800 | AD 1900 | AD 2000 |

WHAT'S THE MEANING OF THIS?
A History of Interpretation

by John Adair

The problem with the Bible," quipped a good friend, "is that it has to be interpreted." Reacting in disbelief, I thought, "Wait, the Bible doesn't have any problems. It's inspired by God and therefore without error." Knowing my friend believed likewise, I quickly realized that his point was not that the Bible has problems, but that we who read and interpret it cause problems. Church history is littered with arguments over the reading of texts like Proverbs 8 or John 1. Pick up any Christian book today, and you'll find the author disagreeing with someone's reading of the biblical text. Some of these debates are incredibly significant; they strike at the very heart of the gospel. All of them are based, at some level, in a desire to discover the truth. And they all involve men and women who are limited in their understanding of the truth.

Such a limited understanding can often prove frustrating. Whether it's a conversation with a spouse, a directive from a boss, or a lecture from a teacher, when we don't understand the fullness of someone's conversation, interpreting his or her meaning can be difficult. So when my wife asks me to take out the trash, it's important that we both know what she means: Which trash—bathroom or kitchen? And when—right now or the next time I go out? It's often pretty easy to see how to clear up simple communications between spouses or coworkers, but how does one do that with an ancient text like the Bible?

Christians throughout history have approached Scripture in a variety of ways, hoping to avoid the misunderstandings so common in communication. Each approach was designed to get at the truth the Bible proclaims to us. Some approaches were more helpful than others, but all of these presented here have been held at some point in time by believers committed to the proclamation of the gospel.

The Early Church (AD 30–600)

The earliest Christians, who lived in the period right after Jesus's earthly ministry, interpreted the Scriptures in a simple yet profound way. Because Christ was the center of their faith, it made perfect sense that the Scriptures would, first and foremost, point to Him. So whether Old Testament or New, whether the text mentions Jesus by name or not, Scripture as the written Word of God would somehow project the divine Word Himself, Jesus Christ. Take prophecy, for example. The Old Testament was viewed by many early Christians as a thoroughly prophetic collection of books, fulfilled in the person and work of Christ. One early Christian, Justin Martyr, saw Christological imagery throughout the Old Testament, whether he found Jesus in the intricacies of Psalm 22 or in a more famous passage like Isaiah 7:14.

Eventually, the church developed two different approaches to complement this Christological interpretation. One group, centered at Antioch in Syria, preferred to emphasize a literal approach to reading the Bible. They believed that it was important to bring out the concrete historical realities of the biblical text. And they wanted to teach the events of biblical history as events, with special attention paid to the literary and historical context. The second group tended toward an allegorical reading. These believers emphasized the spiritual meaning behind the historical reality, a meaning that points readers to the doctrine of the church.

The Medieval Church (AD 600–1500)

As the centuries went by, the church continued to develop its approach to interpretation. But instead of just the literal and allegorical, medieval Christians adopted two additional categories: the moral and the anagogical. The moral reading emphasized how Christians needed to live, while the anagogical simply referred to the way that Scripture points toward the future heavenly reality we Christians all anticipate.

Medieval believers didn't argue that some of these four methods of interpretation were valid while others were not. Instead, they adopted all four in a somewhat layered approach. They saw the literal interpretation as the foundation of a fuller and more mature understanding of the Scriptures, an understanding that came into its fullness only as they embraced all four readings.

Interpreters in the Middle Ages also drew on the early church fathers for direction in their reading of the Bible. They compiled the *catena*, a list of earlier interpretations written in the margins of the biblical text. This illustrates the dual authority of Scripture and tradition given during this period of the church's history.

The Modern, Post-Reformation Church (AD 1500–present)

The Reformers famously reacted against many of the excesses of the Roman Catholic Church, and in doing so attempted to simplify the process of interpreting the Scriptures. This involved several key emphases.

First, the Reformers made the Bible the final authority in all matters, both theological and moral. Church tradition then took on the subordinate role of informing scriptural interpretation without demanding a certain reading.

Second, with the renewed emphasis on reading and interpreting the Bible, they stripped away the complex methods of interpretation developed in the Middle Ages. The literal and historical sense of the text became paramount. Allegories were recognized, but only when it appeared the author intended such a reading.

Third, the Reformers were also keen on reemphasizing a Christ-centered reading of the Scriptures, much like the earliest church fathers did. For the Reformers, everything in Scripture pointed toward Christ, which is consistent with their principle that Scripture interprets Scripture—the New Testament interprets the Old. While a reading of the church fathers would be helpful, ultimately it was in Scripture where the truth could be found.

Finally, the Reformers believed both in the clarity of the Bible and in its freedom from error. Readers coming to the biblical text could trust and understand the message of Christ within its pages. They emphasized relying on the work of the Holy Spirit to reveal the truth of the gospel contained in the pages of Scripture.

These principles of interpretation from the Reformation seek to combine the best of history with a strong emphasis on the primacy of Scripture. We would do well today to heed their call, particularly toward a more Christ-centered approach to reading the Bible.

THE WORD OF GOD AND THE GOD OF THE WORD

The sixty-six divinely inspired books of the Bible represent a diverse collection of writings on a variety of topics, but they are tied together by one common thread—Jesus Christ. Tracing the person and work of Christ through Scripture is a remarkably helpful way to study the Bible, illuminating truth that is highly applicable to the Christian life. Consider the following chart, which briefly describes each book and then examines the presence of Christ within it.

Pentateuch (Legal)

The first five books of the Bible, known as the Pentateuch, were written by Moses and trace the history of the nation of Israel.

	The Book at a Glance	Christ in Scripture
Genesis	Genesis outlines Creation and the beginning of humankind and of Israel, specifically chronicling the lives of Adam, Noah, Abraham, Isaac, Jacob, and Joseph.	Predicted in the seed of the woman (Genesis 3:15); typified by Adam, Melchizedek, and Joseph. See Galatians 4:4; 1 Corinthians 15:22; Hebrews 5:6
Exodus	Exodus describes the "going out" of Israel from Egypt and their struggles to obey a holy God who wanted to dwell with them.	Pictured in the Passover lamb; illustrated by the sacrificial offerings, tabernacle, and articles of worship; typified by Moses and the high priest. See 1 Corinthians 5:7; Hebrews 9:11.
Leviticus	Leviticus, God's guidebook, offers the newly redeemed Israel the way to worship, serve, and gain access to God.	Pictured in the sacrifices and rituals; anticipated as the final, ultimate sacrifice to end all sacrifices. See Ephesians 5:2; Hebrews 10:4–5.

The Book at a Glance	Christ in Scripture
Numbers Numbers transitions God's people from their wilderness wanderings to their place in a new land by illustrating the divine consequences of rebellion.	Predicted in Balaam's prophecy (Numbers 24:17); pictured as manna, water from the rock, and bronze serpent. See John 3:14; 6:31–33; 1 Corinthians 10:4.
Deuteronomy Deuteronomy, meaning "second law," records the recitation of the Law for a new generation of Israel, stressing the importance of loving God and obeying Him with the whole heart.	Predicted as the coming Prophet like Moses (Deuteronomy 18:15); typified by Moses. See John 1:17; Hebrews 3:3.

Historical

The Historical books trace key events in Israel's turbulent history from the time they conquered the land, through their spiritual and political downfall, and finally, to their return from Exile.

The Book at a Glance	Christ in Scripture
Joshua Joshua chronicles the military campaign to reclaim Israel's land; however, they learn that victory is found through faith in God alone.	Typified by Joshua, whose name is the same as "Jesus"; anticipated by Rahab, an ancestor of Christ. See Matthew 1:5.
Judges Judges records the downward spiral of Israel when everyone did what was right in his or her own eyes.	Anticipated in the cycles of sin and deliverance as the ultimate, perfect Judge and Deliverer. See Isaiah 11:4; 2 Timothy 4:1, 8.
Ruth Ruth tells the beautiful love story between King David's great-grandparents and affirms that God will provide for and protect His children.	Typified in Boaz, the kinsman-redeemer, who redeemed Ruth; anticipated by Ruth, an ancestor of Christ. See Matthew 1:5; 1 Peter 1:18.
1 Samuel 1 Samuel chronicles the transition from the judges to the kings, detailing the tragic life of King Saul and rise of King David, demonstrating that though leaders and nations change, God's purposes prevail.	Typified in the life of Samuel (who was prophet, priest, and judge); and the life of David (who was shepherd and king). See 1 Peter 5:4.

	The Book at a Glance	Christ in Scripture
2 Samuel	2 Samuel tells the story of Israel's great King David, a man after God's own heart, who both triumphs in obedience and struggles in disobedience.	Predicted as the Son of David who will rule on David's throne forever (2 Samuel 7:16); typified in David's reign. See Luke 1:32.
1 Kings	1 Kings describes the famous reign of Solomon, whose heart was divided between heavenly and worldly pursuits, and whose reign ended with the division of the kingdom between Israel in the north and Judah in the south.	Typified by Solomon's great wisdom; anticipated by the ministry of Elijah, a type of John the Baptist, who announced the coming of Christ. See Matthew 11:14; 1 Corinthians 1:30.
2 Kings	2 Kings traces the downward fall and destruction of the kingdoms of Israel and Judah, as well as the rise of the prophets who called the people to holiness.	Typified by some faithful kings of Judah; anticipated by the ministry of the prophets. See Luke 9:19.
1 Chronicles	1 Chronicles reviews the history of God's people from the Creation of the world to the creation of the kingdom of Israel, emphasizing God's election of Israel and faithfulness to His covenant.	Predicted in the covenant with David (1 Chronicles 17); typified by the reign of David. See Luke 1:32.
2 Chronicles	2 Chronicles mirrors the history of 2 Kings, concentrating on the spiritual lives of Judah's kings and illustrating God's faithfulness to His eternal promises to David and his descendants.	Typified by the building of the temple and the presence of God with His people. See Matthew 1:23; John 2:19–21; Revelation 21:22.
Ezra	Ezra follows the exiled people's return to the land as God promised and describes a new beginning for Israel.	Anticipated in the preservation of the descendants of David, especially Zerubbabel, an ancestor of Christ; typified by the rebuilding of the temple in Jerusalem. See Matthew 1:13; John 2:19–21.
Nehemiah	Nehemiah outlines the administrative genius and faith of a man who would rally God's people to rebuild the protective walls of Jerusalem.	Typified by Nehemiah, who leaves an exalted position to identify with the plight of his people and lead them to restoration, only to be exalted again. See Philippians 2:5–9.

	The Book at a Glance	Christ in Scripture
Esther	Esther, set during the time of Ezra, tells the story of how God delivered His people from a plot to destroy the Jewish people in Persia.	Typified by Esther's role as the advocate, whose self-sacrificial actions on behalf of her people reversed the law of death. See Romans 8:2; 1 John 2:1.

Wisdom (Poetry)

Wisdom and Poetry books delve into the very personal issues of walking with God, as well as exploring real-life issues of faith.

	The Book at a Glance	Christ in Scripture
Job	Job records the drama of a godly man who, after losing his health, wealth, family, and status, chose to trust that God was at work behind the scenes.	Anticipated in Job's plea for a Mediator and in his faith in an ultimate Redeemer. See 1 Timothy 2:5; Titus 2:14.
Psalms	Psalms, the hymnbook of the Bible, exalts God as worthy of all praise through songs that continue to be sung to this day.	Predicted as both the suffering Messiah (Psalm 22) and conquering King (Psalm 2; 110); typified by images of the Shepherd, Righteous King, and Savior. See Matthew 27:46; Hebrews 1:13.
Proverbs	Proverbs teaches wisdom for living, using short, pithy statements about everyday aspects of life and relationships.	Typified by the wisdom of God and the way of life wisdom produces. See 1 Corinthians 1:24; Colossians 2:3.
Ecclesiastes	Ecclesiastes outlines Solomon's intense search for the meaning of life, ultimately finding it in fearing and obeying God.	Anticipated as the One Shepherd (Ecclesiastes 12:11), who offers a meaningful, abundant life. See John 10:10–15.
Song of Solomon	Song of Solomon details the intimacies of marital love.	Mirrors the bridegroom, who loves and cherishes his wife. See Ephesians 5:25–32.

Prophetic

The Prophetic books foretold the consequences of Israel's refusal to live by God's Word. They condemned man's sinfulness but also assured Israel of God's mercy.

	The Book at a Glance	Christ in Scripture
Isaiah	Isaiah condemns Judah for their sin and predicts God's judgment but also offers comfort in God's faithful, future blessing.	Predicted in the virgin birth (Isaiah 7:14), the Davidic King (9:6–7), the shoot from the stem of Jesse (11:1–5), and the Suffering Servant (52:13–53:12). See Matthew 1:23; Luke 4:17–21; 1 Peter 2:21–25.
Jeremiah	Jeremiah describes Judah at the depth of spiritual decay and announces the heartbreaking news of God's judgment in light of His holiness.	Predicted as the Righteous Branch and the Lord Our Righteousness (Jeremiah 23:5–6); anticipated in the new covenant (31:31–34). See Luke 22:20; 2 Corinthians 5:21.
Lamentations	Lamentations calls the people of Israel to mourn in a prophetic funeral liturgy for Jerusalem, a prophecy that came true forty years later.	Typified by Jeremiah weeping over the sins of Jerusalem and its coming judgment. See Matthew 23:27–38; Luke 13:34–35; 19:41–42.
Ezekiel	Ezekiel administers hope to exiles in Babylon that God's name would be honored and that His glory would not be forgotten.	Predicted as the tender twig that becomes a stately cedar (Ezekiel 17:22–24); anticipated as the ultimate caring Shepherd and in the glory of God returning to the temple in Jerusalem. See Luke 19:43–48; John 10:11.
Daniel	Daniel assures Israel and the world that God is sovereign and will work in the lives of individuals as well as in history, according to His own will.	Predicted as the Stone that will crush the earthly kingdoms (Daniel 2:34–35, 44), the coming Son of Man (7:13–14), and the coming Messiah who will be "cut off" (9:25–26). See Matthew 25:31–32; Mark 13:26.

	The Book at a Glance	Christ in Scripture
Hosea	Hosea's life story symbolizes God's faithfulness and the spiritual adultery of Israel by his marrying and loving a prostitute.	Typified by Israel's call out of Egypt and Hosea's redemption of Gomer from the slave market. See Matthew 2:15; 1 Corinthians 6:20.
Joel	Joel's "day of the Lord" describes Israel's present disaster and future tribulation, but also promises hope and salvation for those who believe.	Typified in the coming of the Lord in both salvation and judgment, which looks forward to the ultimate day of the Lord. See Acts 2:16–21; 1 Thessalonians 5:2.
Amos	Amos foretells judgment coming to Israel in spite of the prosperity they now enjoy and urges them to turn back to the Lord before it is too late.	Typified as the coming Judge who alone has authority to execute judgment and restore His people. See James 4:12.
Obadiah	Obadiah retells the ancient rivalry between Esau and Jacob in the new context of Edom warring—and losing—against Israel.	Typified as the One who judges the enemies of God and comes to His people's aid. See Acts 17:30–31.
Jonah	Jonah emphasizes God's grace in giving wicked people an opportunity to respond to the Word and will of God, teaching lessons to Jonah along the way.	Typified in Jonah's three days in the fish, corresponding to Christ's death and resurrection, and the universal application of God's mercy toward the nations. See Matthew 12:39–41; Mark 16:15–16.
Micah	Micah's message of judgment echoes in a sin-saturated society where justice is absent, but to which the divine Deliverer will be coming.	Predicted in the announcement of the Messiah's birth in Bethlehem (Micah 5:2) and His righteous reign over all the earth (2:12–13; 4:1–8; 5:4–5). See Matthew 2:5–6; Revelation 20:4.

	The Book at a Glance	Christ in Scripture
Nahum	Nahum, meaning "comfort," offers encouragement to Israel that the Assyrians would not go unpunished for their wickedness toward God's people.	Anticipated in the promise to judge the enemies of Israel and to free God's people once and for all. See Acts 1:6.
Habakkuk	Habakkuk tells of the personal struggle the prophet felt with God's plan to judge Israel using a more wicked nation; his resolution is to wait and trust God.	Anticipated in the promise that "the righteous will live by his faith" (Habakkuk 2:4) and "the knowledge of the glory of the Lord" (2:14). See Romans 1:17; 2 Peter 1:3–4.
Zephaniah	Zephaniah speaks of both the wrath and mercy of God for Israel and Gentile nations, for both the present and the future.	Anticipated as the One who preserves the remnant of Israel and rules the earth as King of Israel. See Romans 11:26; Revelation 14:1–3.
Haggai	Haggai rouses enthusiasm for the rebuilding of the second temple and calls people to renewed courage, holiness, and faith in God.	Anticipated by reference to the new temple's "latter glory" and to the One who brings peace (Haggai 2:9). See Matthew 12:6; Ephesians 2:14.
Zechariah	Zechariah challenges people to look ahead in God's plan and see the benefit of their work in rebuilding the temple.	Predicted as the Righteous Branch (Zechariah 3:8; 6:12–13); the Cornerstone, tent peg, and bow of battle (10:4); the Good Shepherd (11:4–13); the pierced One (12:10); and the coming Judge and Righteous King (14:1–21). See John 10:11; 19:37.
Malachi	Malachi urges Israel to be faithful in spite of their questions regarding God's love and protection of His people, pointing them forward to the coming Savior.	Predicted as the One who will fulfill God's covenant with Israel (Malachi 3:1), judge sinners (3:2–5), and bring healing to those who fear the Lord (4:2). See Revelation 20:12.

Biographical (Gospels)

As the fulfillment of the Old Testament, the Gospels, along with the book of Acts, provide the historical and theological backdrop for the rest of the New Testament. Together, they provide a composite picture of the work and person of our Lord Jesus Christ.

	The Book at a Glance	Christ in Scripture
Matthew	Matthew presents the birth, teachings, life, death, and resurrection of Christ for a Hebrew audience, highlighting Jesus's continuity with Old Testament Scripture.	Jesus is the King, the long-awaited Messiah, who fulfills the prophecies, promises, types, and expectations of the Old Testament Scriptures. See Matthew 16:16–19; 28:18–20.
Mark	Mark presents the life and teachings of Jesus from Peter's perspective, for a primarily Roman audience, focusing on the suffering and death of Christ for sin.	Jesus is the Suffering Servant who gives His life to save the world. See Mark 10:45.
Luke	Luke, the physician, presents a well-researched and orderly account of Christ's genealogy, birth, teachings, death, and resurrection, trying to convince an intellectual reader of the divine origins of the Christian faith.	Jesus is the perfect, ideal God-man who comes to offer salvation to all humankind—Jew and Gentile alike. See Luke 19:10.
John	John, the beloved disciple, presents his eyewitness account of the life and teachings of Jesus in order to convince his readers that Jesus is the Messiah, the divine and human Son of God and Savior of the world.	Jesus is the Christ, the Son of God, the way, the truth, and the life who alone is the revelation of God and salvation of people. See John 1:1–18; 20:31.

Historical

	The Book at a Glance	Christ in Scripture
Acts	Acts paints a historical portrait of the earliest years of the church, from Jesus's ascension to Paul's missionary travels, highlighting God's plan to reach both Jews and Gentiles with the good news of salvation.	Jesus is the glorified, enthroned Savior who continues His ministry in the world by means of the Holy Spirit working through His disciples until He returns. See Acts 1:7–9.

Doctrinal (Letters)

For the first time, God used personal letters as a vehicle for divine inspiration. These letters, most of which were written by the apostle Paul, addressed specific problems and issues that have timeless and universal application.

	The Book at a Glance	Christ in Scripture
Romans	Romans explains the significance of Jesus's death, clarifies what it takes to be accepted by God, and illustrates how to live a godly life.	Jesus is the focus of the gospel and the means of salvation by God's grace apart from works. See Romans 1:1–4, 16–17.
1 Corinthians	1 Corinthians addresses a variety of problems that faced the early church: moral and ethical, doctrinal and practical, and corporate and private.	Jesus is the source of unity among believers who are baptized into the body of Christ and the basis of their ultimate resurrection and glorification. See 1 Corinthians 12:12–13; 15.
2 Corinthians	2 Corinthians rejoices that the church in Corinth had experienced a change in heart and was now accepting Paul and each other in their God-given roles.	Jesus is the One who comforts us in our suffering, reconciles us to God, and gives strength in our weaknesses. See 2 Corinthians 1:5; 5:17–21; 12:9.
Galatians	Galatians urges believers not to give up their freedom in Christ in exchange for either loose living or legalism.	Jesus is the source and power of the believer's new life and the heir of the promises to Abraham's seed. See Galatians 2:20; 3:16.
Ephesians	Ephesians reminds believers of the great spiritual wealth that is theirs because of their inheritance in Christ.	Jesus is the source of spiritual blessings, the Cornerstone of the church, and the goal of spiritual maturity. See Ephesians 1:3; 2:20; 4:11–16.
Philippians	Philippians urges believers to focus their lives on the joy and encouragement found in Christ, regardless of their circumstances.	Jesus is the Son of God from heaven who humbled Himself by becoming human, suffered for us, and was exalted to heaven. See Philippians 2:5–11.

	The Book at a Glance	Christ in Scripture
Colossians	Colossians affirms the supremacy of the person of Jesus Christ and the completeness of the salvation that He provides.	Jesus is our supreme Lord of the church and the world, the all-sufficient Savior in whom the fullness of deity dwells. See Colossians 1:13–20, 2:9.
1 Thessalonians	1 Thessalonians calls believers to excel in their faith and love for one another and to always be thankful.	Jesus is our source of hope and comfort, the One who rescues believers from the coming wrath. See 1 Thessalonians 1:10; 4:13–5:11.
2 Thessalonians	2 Thessalonians comforts believers who are suffering and urges them to continue trusting God in light of future events.	Jesus is the coming Judge who will reward the righteous and destroy the wicked, including the coming man of lawlessness in the end times. See 2 Thessalonians 1:6–2:12.
1 Timothy	1 Timothy directs leaders in how to conduct themselves, guard against false doctrine, and develop mature leadership in the church.	Jesus is the Mediator between God and people, the ransom for all, who came in the flesh and was taken up in glory. See 1 Timothy 2:5–6; 3:16.
2 Timothy	2 Timothy, the final letter written by Paul, pictures a very personal portrait of what it means to finish well and remain faithful to the very end.	Jesus is the Judge of the living and the dead, who strengthens us in times of weakness and rescues us in times of danger. See 2 Timothy 3:11; 4:1, 17
Titus	Titus offers practical wisdom for church organization and leadership, emphasizing good works as an evidence of true faith.	Jesus is our great God and Savior, who redeems and purifies His people. See Titus 2:13–14.
Philemon	Philemon asks a slave owner to extend forgiveness to a runaway slave because of the grace extended to him in Christ.	Jesus is the Master, in whom believers are brothers and sisters in Christ. See Philemon 9, 15–16.
Hebrews	Hebrews appeals to Jewish believers who, because of great persecution, wanted to turn back to Judaism.	Jesus is the absolutely superior revelation of God and our eternal High Priest. See Hebrews 1; 3:1.

	The Book at a Glance	Christ in Scripture
James	James integrates true faith and everyday practical living by saying faith is visible in the way we choose to live our lives.	Jesus is the glorious Lord who inspires true faith and authentic works. See James 2:1, 14–26.
1 Peter	1 Peter illustrates that persecution can cause us to grow or grumble, so we can choose whether hard times will develop—or destroy—our character.	Jesus is the living stone rejected by men, who has become the Cornerstone of the church and the Shepherd of our souls. See 1 Peter 2:4–10, 25.
2 Peter	2 Peter reminds believers of the timeless truths of the faith and encourages them to continue growing through spiritual maturity.	Jesus is the Morning Star, who rescues the righteous from temptation and reserves the wicked for judgment. See 2 Peter 1:19; 2:9.
1 John	1 John explores the relationship between God and His people in terms of light, love, and eternal life.	Jesus is the Word of Life, who is God come in the flesh to bring eternal life to those who believe. See 1 John 1:1; 4:2; 5:20.
2 John	2 John affirms that Christians should love each other, but warns that hospitality shouldn't be extended to those wanting to destroy the truth.	Jesus is the Son of the Father, who alone is the way to the Father. See 2 John 3, 9.
3 John	3 John commends believers who are making their faith an active part of their lives and godly character their priority.	Jesus is the Name, for whose sake believers minister. See 3 John 7–8.
Jude	Jude reveals the true nature of false teachers and encourages believers to fight for the faith.	Jesus is our only Master and Lord, who will judge the false prophets at His coming. See Jude 4, 14–16.

Prophetic

Revelation completes God's story, begun in Genesis, with a dramatic description of God's plan for the end of the world.

	The Book at a Glance	Christ in Scripture
Revelation	With vivid, descriptive terms, the apostle John records a God-given vision of His plan for the end of the present world and the beginning of a new world.	Jesus is the coming King of kings and Lord of lords, who will return as Judge and King to usher in the kingdom of God on earth. See Revelation 19:11–20:6.

FASCINATING FACTS

- The longest chapter in the Bible is Psalm 119 (176 verses).

- The shortest chapter is Psalm 117 (two verses).

- The longest verse in the Bible is Esther 8:9 (more than eighty words).

- The shortest verse is John 11:35 (two words).

- The longest book in the Old Testament is Psalms.

- The shortest book in the Old Testament is Obadiah (twenty-one verses).

- The longest book in the New Testament is Luke.

- The shortest book in the New Testament is 2 John (thirteen verses).

- One of the oddest verses in the Bible is 1 Chronicles 26:18. (Look it up!)

- Other than the word *the*, the word most often used in the Bible is *Lord*.

- The two longest words in the Bible (it's a tie) read: *Jonath-elem-rechokim* (Psalm 56), meaning "a silent dove of far off lands." And *Maher-shalal-hash-baz* (Isaiah 8:3), the name of Isaiah's son, which means "quick to the plunder, swift to the spoil."

HOW TO STUDY THE *Bible*

THIS WE BELIEVE
Basic Doctrines for Biblical Discernment

by Michael J. Svigel

I recently came across a person who had cut himself off from all churches and doctrinal accountability, having decided to base his doctrine and practice on his own independent study of the Bible. Forget theology! Forget centuries of God-gifted teachers! He alone—with the Bible alone—would be the sole formulator of true teaching. What was the result? Among other major doctrinal deviations, he concluded that *the city of Jerusalem is God* . . . based on a "literal" reading of Psalm 48:12–14! He did not care at all that no other believer in history had ever taught such a thing or that this interpretation radically altered the concept of God Himself. The Bible "said" it, so he believed it!

While we base our doctrine on the Bible, trusting it as our final, inerrant authority, those who are prideful and untrained in Scripture are liable to go astray from a right interpretation of the Bible. Believers can avoid all kinds of theological and practical errors by understanding the central Christian doctrines that defined the faith even before the church had an official, complete collection of New Testament writings to study. In fact, the apostle Peter warned that "the untaught and unstable" distort the Scriptures "to their own destruction" (2 Peter 3:16). That's a serious warning. The solution? Be taught!

It is vital to have an understanding of the basic, essential beliefs of the Christian faith and to know where those doctrines are taught in the Bible. An awareness of these teachings will prevent a person from ignorantly or arrogantly reading the Bible in a way that contradicts the Christian faith and leads to destruction. Learning biblical doctrine from God-gifted teachers brings stability (see Matthew 28:20; Ephesians 4:11–16; 2 Timothy 2:2).

While diversity has always been characteristic of a vibrant and vital Christianity, all true Christians agree on the essentials of their common faith. The following ten statements reflect these essential biblical doctrines as understood by the ministry of Insight for Living.

The Bible — *We affirm our confidence in God's inerrant Word. We treasure its truths, and we respect its reproofs.*

The sixty-six books of the Old and New Testaments are the Word of God, inspired by the Holy Spirit, and written centuries ago by chosen men of God. The Bible is without error in its original manuscripts, is completely reliable as the final authority in all matters of doctrine and practice, and is centered on the person and work of Jesus Christ. See 1 Thessalonians 2:13; 2 Timothy 3:15–17; and 2 Peter 1:20–21.

God the Father — *We acknowledge the Creator-God as our heavenly Father, infinitely perfect and intimately acquainted with all our ways.*

As the first person of the Trinity, the Father is the source and ruler of all things and is fatherly in His relationship with creation in general and believers in particular. And although there is one eternal, all-powerful, all-knowing, holy, just, loving, true, and unchangeable God, in the unity of the one God there are three divine persons — Father, Son, and Holy Spirit — equal in power but distinct in roles. See Psalm 103:19; Matthew 28:19; and 1 Peter 1:2.

The Lord Jesus Christ — *We claim Jesus Christ as our Lord — the very God who came in human flesh — the object of our worship and the subject of our praise.*

As the second person of the Trinity, the Son reveals the Father. According to the Father's plan, the eternal Son humbled Himself and became incarnate, inseparably uniting undiminished deity with true humanity. As fully God and fully man, Jesus Christ lived a sinless life, died to pay in full the penalty for our sin, rose bodily and miraculously from the dead, ascended into heaven, and will come again in glory. See John 1:1–3, 14; Philippians 2:5–8; Hebrews 1:1–3; and 1 John 5:11–12.

The Holy Spirit—*We recognize the Holy Spirit as the third member of the Godhead who is incessantly at work convicting, convincing, and comforting.*

As the third person of the Trinity, the Holy Spirit is the personal agent of the Father and Son for revelation and regeneration. Though pervasively present and active in creation, the Holy Spirit specially dwells among God's people and uniquely indwells individual believers, giving them new life and empowering them for lives of personal holiness. See John 14:26; Acts 1:5, 8; 1 Corinthians 6:19–20; and Ephesians 1:13–14.

The Depravity of Humanity—*We confess that Adam's fall into sin left humanity without the hope of heaven apart from a new birth made possible by the Savior's substitutionary death and miraculous, bodily resurrection.*

As a result of Adam's rebellion, all people have fallen under the curse of death. Unable and unwilling to please God, all humans are undeserving of His blessings, blinded to His truth, and dead in their sins—spiritually and, ultimately, physically. This state of judgment before the just and holy God is a condition that permeates every facet of human life and cannot be cured apart from the grace of God through Christ. See Genesis 3; Jeremiah 17:9; and Romans 3:10–18, 23; 5:12.

Salvation—*We believe the offer of salvation is God's love-gift to all. Those who accept it by faith, apart from works, become new creatures in Christ.*

Because fallen humans are unable to save themselves, God, according to His own sovereign mercy, acts to save those who come to Him by grace through faith. God sent His Son, Jesus Christ, to suffer the penalty of death in place of condemned humanity. Simply through believing the good news that Christ died for his or her sins and then rose from the dead, a person can be forgiven of all sin, declared righteous by God, reborn into new life, and guaranteed eternal life with God. See John 3:16; Romans 10:9–10; 1 Corinthians 15:1–5; and Ephesians 1:4–12; 2:8–9.

The Return of Christ—*We anticipate our Lord's promised return, which could occur at any moment.*

According to the Father's plan, Jesus Christ will one day return in power to bring completion of salvation and rewards to believers and judgment and wrath to unbelievers. The Bible teaches that the years leading up to the judgment will be marked by increasing evil, but the actual time of the end is unknown. It could begin at any moment. Though the details of Christ's return are sometimes unclear, its reality is certain, and all believers are called to live holy lives in anticipation of His coming. See 1 Thessalonians 4:13–5:11; 2 Thessalonians 2:1–12; Hebrews 9:28; and Revelation 19:11–16.

Resurrection of Humanity—*We are convinced that all who have died will be brought back from beyond—believers to everlasting communion with God and unbelievers to everlasting separation from God.*

Though a believer's spirit is ushered into the Lord's presence immediately upon physical death, the fullness of salvation awaits Christ's return, when He will resurrect believers in glorified bodies like His own immortal body which can never die. While all believers throughout history will enjoy eternal life in perfect paradise, unbelievers will be resurrected to suffer eternal conscious punishment for their sins. See John 11:23–27; 1 Corinthians 15:51–57; 1 Thessalonians 4:13–18; and Revelation 20:4–21:5.

The Body of Christ—*We know the Lord is continuing to enlarge His family, the universal body of Christ, over which He rules as Head.*

The body of Christ is the ever-enlarging universal church consisting of true believers in heaven and on earth over whom Jesus Christ reigns as Lord. Regardless of denomination, all true believers are spiritually baptized by the Holy Spirit into Christ's body and are therefore spiritually united with Him and with one another. See Romans 12:4–5; 1 Corinthians 12:12–14; Ephesians 4:11–16; and 1 Peter 2:9–10.

The Family of God — *We are grateful to be a part of the local church, which exists to proclaim God's truth, to administer the ordinances, to stimulate growth toward maturity, and to bring glory to God.*

Believers are called to faithful membership in a visible, local congregation for the purpose of mutual encouragement and spiritual growth. As the family of God, a healthy local church is marked by God-glorifying worship, Scripture-centered teaching, intimate fellowship, and vivid expressions of the church's faith, hope, and love through evangelism, disciple-making, financial support, and service. See Acts 2:41–47; Philippians 2:1–4; and Hebrews 10:24–25.

THE TRINITY

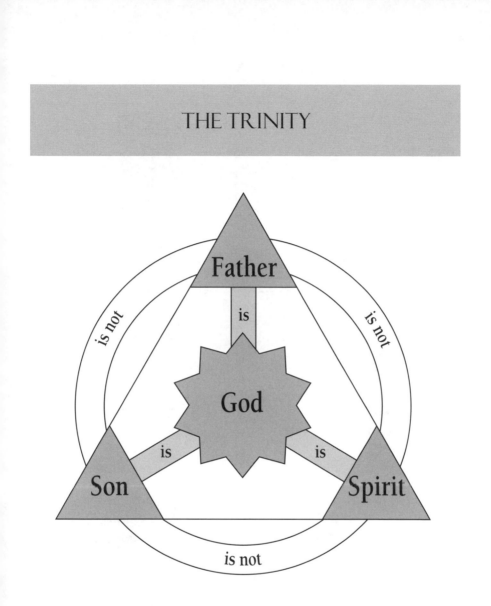

The Bible

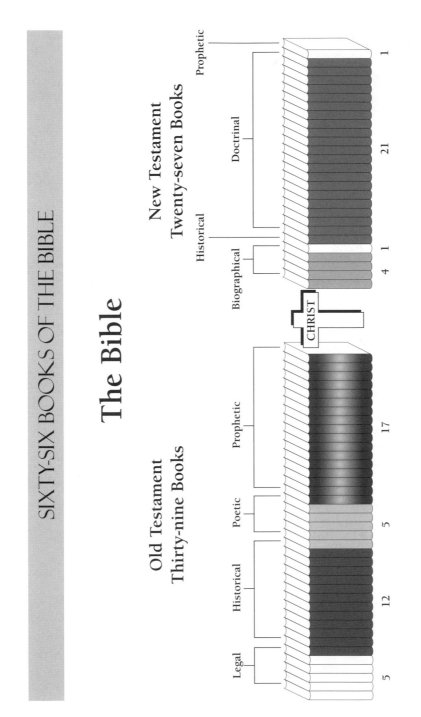

Old Testament
Thirty-nine Books

Legal — 5
Historical — 12
Poetic — 5
Prophetic — 17

CHRIST

New Testament
Twenty-seven Books

Biographical — 4
Historical — 1
Doctrinal — 21
Prophetic — 1

SURVEY OF THE BIBLE BOOKS

Creation, Fall, Flood, Babel, Patriarchs, Bondage, Deliverance, Law, Wanderings, Conquest of Canaan, and Compromise

Books:
Genesis (Beginnings)
Job (Suffering)
Exodus (Deliverance)
Leviticus (Worship)
Numbers (Wanderings)
Deuteronomy (Remember)
Joshua (Conquest)
Judges (Defeat)
Ruth (Love)

Samuel, Saul, David, Solomon

United Kingdom

Books:
1 Samuel 1–
1 Kings 11
Psalms
Proverbs
Ecclesiastes
Song of Solomon

Northern (Israel)

Books:
Jonah
Amos
Hosea

Divided Kingdom

1 Kings 12 –
2 Chronicles 36

Southern (Judah)

Invasion by Assyria (722 BC)

Exile in Babylon (586 BC – 516 BC)

Books of the Prophets:

Preexilic
Obadiah
Joel
Isaiah
Micah

Nahum
Habakkuk
Zephaniah
Jeremiah

Exilic
Lamentations
Ezekiel
Daniel

Returns

1. Zerubbabel
2. Ezra
3. Nehemiah

Restoration

Postexilic
Haggai
Zechariah
Malachi

Other Books
Ezra
Nehemiah
Esther

Between the Testaments – 400 Silent Years
(No Scripture written)

John the Baptizer
Lord Jesus Christ
Disciples

Apostles and Beginning of the Church

Books:
Matthew (King)
Mark (Servant)
Luke (Man)
John (God)
Acts
Epistles
Revelation

PRINCIPLES AND PEOPLE
Biographical and Topical Studies

by Barb Peil, Wendy Peterson, and Derrick G. Jeter

Studying and applying God's Word can take a number of forms. Besides reading and reflecting on a particular book of the Bible, such as Proverbs or the Gospel of John, you can also seek God's counsel for practical living by studying the accounts of people in the Bible or exploring what the Bible teaches on particular topics. In the following sections, we've outlined some basic steps for doing biographical and topical studies, to help you get the most out of your time in God's Word.

How to Study a Biblical Biography

God is the greatest storyteller of all time. With epic narratives like Job that begin, "There was a man in the land of Uz" (Job 1:1), we are plucked out of our world and dropped into another. Suddenly we're in a different time and culture, and yet the people we meet face challenges, disappointments, relationships, and crises of faith like ours. As we study their lives, they emerge from the two-dimensional world on the page to become real flesh-and-blood. They're living models of faith (Hebrews 11), and no matter how many times we read their stories, we see afresh God working in and through individual lives — no matter the time or place.

Learn about your character's world. Where did this person live? How did the geographical location affect his life? When did this person live? What events coincided with her life? What attitudes, beliefs, and customs prevailed in the world at this time? Observe every detail available about the political, geographical, and religious climate of his time. The better we understand her world, the more accurately and vividly we'll see God at work in her life.

89

Use every relevant detail in the story to get to know his or her personality and character. What do you know about his physical appearance? How do other characters respond to her? What are his recorded thoughts and words? What do her actions say about her? Is he mentioned elsewhere in Scripture? What do others say about her?

Identify the conflict that the person faces. Is he or she facing the temptation to disobey a moral or godly command? Is there disharmony in his family or community? Does the battle rage primarily within her own heart? Is he in a conflict with another character? Is she struggling to trust God in life's ordinary events or extraordinary catastrophes?

When we see our own experiences in an individual's tests of faith, his or her story can serve as a model of a spiritual truth. The way he responded to his tests of faith becomes pivotal to the development of his character. The same is true today for us. How is your test of faith similar to what she faced? What does the fact that God provided this person's life as an example say about God's character? What does it say about your faith, trust, or obedience to God? What principle have you learned from this person's life that you can apply to your life?

The process of a biographical study is simple. As you read the passage, write down some basic observations. Then read a few Bible commentaries, handbooks, and books on biblical culture to discover more about the world of your chosen individual. Read other Scripture sections where this person is mentioned. Then draw parallels between the conflicts and lessons this person faced and the ones that you now encounter. In so doing, you will transform the "Long ago and far away" to "There once was a man or a woman who faced the same kind of test as I do . . . and God was faithful to him or her. And He will be faithful to me." After all, these stories are not just about people, but about what God did to and through ordinary people like you and me. God is the hero of every story—including yours.

How to Do a Topical Bible Study

God is so gracious to share His wise counsel with us! Through His Word and His Spirit's guidance, we can learn to follow His ways in all aspects of life.

But where do we start? The Bible can seem so vast, so impenetrable. A systematic, book-by-book study beginning with Genesis and ending with Revelation can be an overwhelming task when we need God's particular word at this moment in our lives. This is when choosing a theme—like money, anger, family relationships, justice, or helping the poor—can best bring us in touch with God's wisdom.

By tracing a single topic through Scripture, we integrate God's teaching throughout time and in a variety of settings. Exploring a subject from many different angles provides us with a more complete, well-rounded picture—and a clearer, more comprehensive response.

A thematic study requires certain tools. These include a reliable Bible translation, such as the New American Standard Bible (NASB), with plenty of cross-references; a concordance or Bible software that matches your Bible translation; and a topical Bible, such as *Nave's* or *The Handbook of Bible Application*, which can give you a head start because it has already arranged Scripture under a comprehensive variety of topics. A Bible dictionary and Bible encyclopedia will also come in handy, as will a user-friendly systematic theology, if you're studying a particular doctrine (see "Resources for Digging Deeper" on page 125).

Now that we've gathered our tools, here's a simple way to do a thematic study.

Pray. Ask the Lord to guide you and help you be receptive to what He wants to teach you.

Brainstorm. If you want to study God's perspective on money, for instance, some other words you'll want to look up in the concordance or search for in your Bible software are *riches*, *wealth*, or *gold*.

Focus. After examining the Bible passages you've found, cull out the peripheral verses and record the more direct passages—those that deal with your topic of interest specifically and in greater detail.

Organize. Group passages that make a similar point, trying to discover which passages are more central and clear, which offer secondary information, and which provide illustrations to follow.

Meditate. Read and reread the passages you've chosen, perhaps in different versions to expand your insight. What are they saying in context? Discover how separate passages connect, and ponder why God said the things He has said.

Write. Make notes about what you find throughout the process. Also, as you jot down your references, summarize what the verses say and interpret what they mean. Record questions you have and any answers you find. Integrate what you learn by writing it down.

Apply. Think through questions such as, What does this teach about God's nature? His purpose? How will this work itself out in my life?

The Lord's wisdom "is more precious than jewels," Solomon tells us, "and nothing you desire compares with her" (Proverbs 3:15). Let's partake of His counsel, then—we'll be immeasurably richer for it!

FASCINATING FACTS

- The ten most-mentioned women in the Bible are:

    Sarah, Abraham's wife, fifty-six times

    Rachel, Jacob's second wife, forty-seven times

    Leah, Jacob's first wife, thirty-four times

    Rebekah, Isaac's wife, thirty-one times

    Jezebel, wicked queen and wife of Ahab, twenty-three times

    Mary, Jesus's mother, nineteen times

    Abigail, Nabal's wife and then King David's wife, fifteen times

    Miriam, Moses and Aaron's sister, fifteen times

    Mary Magdalene, Jesus's friend, fourteen times

    Hagar, Abraham's concubine, fourteen times

- Eve, the mother of the human race, is mentioned only four times!

BIBLICAL GARDENING
Tips on Preparing and Leading a Bible Study
by Derrick G. Jeter

G rowing up, my sisters and I often spent weekends at my grandfather's farm. He wasn't a farmer by trade, but he had a little patch of dirt where he raised cattle and vegetables. Being required to work in the garden, I learned the value of sharp tools, a cultivated field, healthy seed, and plentiful water, not only to make the labor easier but to reap an abundant crop in the fall.

As I began to study and teach Scripture, I understood that what is true when tending a garden is equally true when preparing and leading Bible studies. The tools, field, seed, and plants are different, but if we wish to gather a bumper spiritual harvest, in ourselves and in others, we must attend to some basic guidelines for successful Bible study.

Sharpening Your Tools

No farmer begins the planting season without first sharpening his equipment. When planting a biblical garden, there are three primary tools you should file to a razor-sharp edge. Howard G. Hendricks, in his helpful volume *Living by the Book*, details these three tools.

First, *observe* the text by asking, What do I see? Read carefully and look for content (facts)—what is said—and for composition (form)—how it's said. Make special note of key persons, places, events, ideas, and times. A helpful acronym can remind you of several key items to observe; so find PEACE:

> Promises to claim (2 Corinthians 1:20; 1 John 2:25)
> Examples to follow (1 Corinthians 10:6; 1 Peter 2:21)
> Attitudes to espouse (Philippians 2:3–5)
> Commands to obey (John 14:15)
> Errors or sins to avoid (1 John 2:4; 4:1)

Once you've jotted down your observations, you might want to manage them in a chart, similar to the one on page 114.

Second, *interpret* the text by asking, What does it mean? The goal here is to bridge the gap between the biblical world and your world. To do so, you must keep in mind that the Bible is a historical book—the authors lived in specific cultural contexts and desired to accomplish certain purposes by employing all the tools of written language. But the Bible is also a divine book containing mystery and doctrine written in literary forms that are sometimes foreign to modern readers. Turn to "Resources for Digging Deeper" on page 125 to find helpful tools for understanding the historical background of authors and audiences; the cultural background; and the literary background of narrative, poetic, wisdom, prophetic, or epistolary form, as well as the grammatical structures and figurative language.

Third, *apply* the text by asking, What difference does it make? To do this appropriately, you must know yourself and the people you lead. One helpful way to get a handle on the application is to state the verse or passage as a succinct, specific, and positive principle. Be careful; make sure the principle is in harmony with the general tenor of Scripture. And another word of warning: you can't apply something to your group that you haven't applied yourself, so make sure you are working to plant and cultivate the principle in your own life first.

Plowing the Field

Once your tools are sharp, there is one more important task you need to take care of before planting the Word of God—you must ready the soil.

Whether for your own edification or in preparation to lead a group study, here are a few recommendations to help you plow the spiritual field.

First, *examine your own life* to be sure you are walking in a close relationship with God. A dirty spiritual life will not only cloud your own understanding of Scripture but also muddy any lessons you try to teach others. Only those who are in a right relationship with God can truly understand and apply the Scriptures to their lives and the lives of others

(1 Corinthians 2:14). This is the native nutrient of all spiritual soil. (If you are unsure about your relationship with God, see "How to Begin a Relationship with God" on page 115.)

Next, *pray, pray, and pray some more*. For yourself and for those you lead, pray for enlightened hearts that know the "hope of His calling" (Ephesians 1:18), for abounding love to "approve the things that are excellent" (Philippians 1:10), and to know God's will so you can "walk in a manner worthy of the Lord" (Colossians 1:10).

Finally, *come to the Scripture with humility* (1 Corinthians 1:26–29) and an obedient heart (Hebrews 5:11–14), trusting the Holy Spirit to guide you (John 14:26).

Planting the Seed

Now, you're ready to plant the seed of God's Word. Your study and obedience should have germinated the seed in your life, but the key to planting in another's life is hard work—you must prepare beforehand (2 Timothy 2:15) and communicate the truth in such a way that your group can understand and learn. You must get to know the group members in your Bible study. What are their backgrounds? Are they believers or not? How long have they been Christians? What are their struggles and triumphs, their joys and sorrows? These and similar questions will help you to know what kind of soil you're working with and help you to determine where to place the seed and how to water it (Mark 4:3–9, 13–20).

Watering the Plants

After planting the seed, you must immediately water it—but not too much, you don't want to wash it away. A gentle shower is all that is needed.

Encourage your group to share their thoughts and feelings. Don't worry if some of their ideas are off the beaten theological path— remember, some in your group may have just had the seed of the gospel planted in their hearts, or they're new, tender shoots. Be flexible, and patiently guide them back to the truth.

Ask open-ended questions and resist the urge to fill the silence or give the "right" answer. Gently challenge your group to think biblically— to look to Scripture to "prove" their points.

Embody the truth in your own life. Nothing will scorch new growth faster than the heat of hypocrisy. But seeing a model of humility and obedience is like a refreshing shower in a parched land.

Create times of fellowship. Occasionally, get together, not to study, but to enjoy time with and pray for one another. Share meals together. This will not only deepen your understanding of the individuals in your group, it will deepen their commitment to the Lord and His Word as they see how He makes a distinctive difference in real life.

Reaping the Harvest

Sharp tools to till the ground, good soil preparation, proper planting, food and water, and patience will reap an abundant spiritual harvest— in yourself and in your group.

Whether you study the Bible in preparation to facilitate a group or simply for your own edification, you'll produce spiritual fruit that is ripe and lush within your own life (Galatians 5:22–23). Your study will enable you to store your knowledge of Scripture, making you mature. It will enable you to confirm your knowledge of Scripture, building your faith. And it will enable you to direct your knowledge of Scripture, defending your faith.

The fruit produced in the lives of others will vary in quality and quantity. Sometimes you won't harvest—you'll only plant or water for others to harvest—but you must remain in the fields and faithfully labor (1 Corinthians 3:4–9). Other times you will harvest new souls for Christ (John 4:35–38) and cause others to grow up in Christ so they may go out into the fields with sharp tools to plow and plant and water and harvest (Ephesians 4:11–12).

This Bible handbook will sharpen your knowledge, but sharp tools never put to use will rust where they stand. The Lord has given us implements to plow, plant, water, and harvest. So as you walk out into the field, may your tools remain sharp and your harvest bountiful.

FASCINATING FACTS

- Nine times God raised people from the dead:

  Elijah raised the son of the Zarephath widow
  (1 Kings 17:17–22)

  Elisha raised the son of the Shunammite woman
  (2 Kings 4:32–35)

  A man was raised from the dead when his body
  touched Elisha's bones (2 Kings 13:20–21)

  Jesus raised the son of the widow of Nain
  (Luke 7:11–15)

  Jesus raised the daughter of Jairus
  (Luke 8:41–55)

  Jesus raised Lazarus after Lazarus had been dead
  for four days (John 11:1–44)

  Many saints rose from the dead at Jesus's death
  (Matthew 27:50–53)

  Peter raised Dorcas (Acts 9:36–41)

  Paul raised Eutychus (Acts 20:9–10)

- One person who was raised by Himself:

  Jesus rose from the dead (Matthew 28:5–9;
  Mark 16:6; Luke 24:5–6) and, unlike any of the
  others listed above, *He never died again.*

A TREASURE WORTH FINDING
Why Study the Bible?

by Wil Luce

The Bible . . . the very words and wisdom of God. What an incredible thought! And it's not the theoretical sort of wisdom intended to merely raise our IQ a few notches. It is practical truth geared to show us how to live our lives successfully. Nothing in this world is of greater value or of more importance than the truth of this book. Solomon wrote:

> If you seek her as silver
> And search for her as for hidden treasures;
> Then you will discern the fear of the LORD
> And discover the knowledge of God. (Proverbs 2:4–5)

Scripture contains the wisdom we need to let us know when we are moving in the wrong direction, to show us how to get back on track, and to teach us how to live as God intended (2 Timothy 3:16–17). And because God is the author, we can be certain His Word is reliable and true.

So why don't we dig into Bible study more than we do? Possibly because our attempts have proven less than spectacular. Though we see others hitting the mother lode of spiritual discovery, we feel that we've come up with little more than fool's gold. We may begin our quest with great enthusiasm, but it usually isn't long before disappointment and discouragement set in. Somehow our efforts often don't meet our expectations.

If this describes your experience, take heart. By adding a few simple skills to your repertoire, Bible study can become the great experience you have heard others talk about. Let's look at a few ideas that will enrich the time you spend in God's Word.

Be Consistent

It's unwise to load up our bodies with a huge meal and then go for a week or two without food. The same is true spiritually. Regularity and consistency are critical. Here are some ideas that might help.

- *Pick a time when you are least likely to be interrupted.* Then, discipline yourself to keep the appointment, even when you don't feel like it.

- *Study in the same location each time, and stay there.* This will help your mind shift into a Bible study mode more quickly.

- *Keep everything you need right at hand.* Your Bible, study books, devotionals, and writing materials should be within reach.

- *Ask God to give you understanding.* The Holy Spirit is the ultimate Teacher, and He will lead you into all truth.

Be Methodical

Without a plan, you'll just be turning shovelfuls of empty dirt. You have to know *where* and *how* to dig, as well as *what* you're looking for. Begin by selecting a passage of interest to you. No matter which passage you begin with, you need a plan. How do you decide *where* to dig?

A good way to approach the New Testament is to begin with one of the four Gospels, perhaps John. Then move through the Historical book of Acts, spend some time in the Doctrinal book of Romans, and then work through the very practical letter to the Galatians. Later, consider the difficult teachings of James, and then tackle Hebrews and 1 John. Now you can return to one of the other three Gospels and proceed from there to pick up some of the books you missed the first time through. Leave Revelation until you have a pretty good grasp of the rest of the Bible. Revelation might be seen as the Grand Central Station of Scripture, where everything comes together. To understand it well, knowledge of all that has come before is needed.

Now, don't forget about the Old Testament. The New Testament is rooted in that part of the Bible. Frequently it portrays New Testament truth in illustrative form. The Legal and Historical books, Genesis through Esther, can be read chronologically for study purposes. For the sake of balance, intersperse one of the Poetic or Wisdom books, Job through Song of Solomon, and include some Prophetic books from time to time as well.

Don't feel bound by these recommendations. The Holy Spirit may prompt you to a different order because of specific issues that surface during the course of your studies. Consider these as suggestions.

Be Thorough

What looks like a worthless dirt clod might conceal a valuable gold nugget. So don't overlook the details within the major themes of a passage. Invest in a few resources. A good study Bible is a great place to begin. These contain abbreviated libraries of information right with the text of Scripture. In addition, you'll want a good concordance and a Bible dictionary. Later, you can add a couple of one-volume commentaries on the entire Bible.

So how do you find those gold nuggets? Glean as much information and understanding of the passage as you can through studying the passage on your own, and then consult what others have written. Use your dictionary and your concordance for better word understanding, but don't turn to the commentaries until you have exhausted your capacity to discern the meaning on your own. Then examine the commentaries to verify and/or correct the conclusions to which you have come.

Now go ahead, grab your gear, and get ready to dig in and explore the hidden reaches of biblical discovery! A commitment to study the Bible is a great sign of spiritual maturity and an indication that you're growing in your walk with the Lord. You will begin to uncover for yourself the priceless gems of biblical truth waiting to be found.

APPENDIX

A COMPARISON OF THE BEGINNING AND THE END[10]

Genesis 1–3	Revelation 20–22
"In the beginning God created the heavens and the earth" (1:1)	"I saw a new heaven and a new earth" (21:1)
"The darkness He called Night" (1:5)	"There shall be no night there" (21:25)
"God made two great lights" (sun and moon; 1:16)	"The city had no need of the sun or of the moon" (21:23)
"In the day that you eat of it you shall surely die" (2:17)	"There shall be no more death" (21:4)
Satan appears as deceiver of mankind (3:1)	Satan disappears forever (20:10)
Shown a garden into which defilement entered (3:6–7)	Shown a city into which defilement will never enter (21:27)
Walk of God with man interrupted (3:8–10)	Walk of God with man resumed (21:3)
Initial triumph of the serpent (3:13)	Ultimate triumph of the Lamb (20:10; 22:3)
"I will greatly multiply your sorrow" (3:16)	"There shall be no more death or sorrow, nor crying; and there shall be no more pain" (21:4)
"Cursed is the ground for your sake" (3:17)	"There shall be no more curse" (22:3)
Man's dominion broken in the fall of the first man, Adam (3:19)	Man's dominion restored in the rule of the new man, Christ (22:5)
First paradise closed (3:23)	New paradise opened (21:25)
Access to the tree of life disinherited in Adam (3:24)	Access to the tree of life reinstated in Christ (22:14)
They were driven from God's presence (3:24)	"They shall see His face" (22:4)

THE PENTATEUCH

Book of the Pentateuch	What It Tells Us about Humanity	What It Tells Us about God
Genesis	Ruin and rebellion through sin	Sovereignty
Exodus	Redemption from bondage	Omnipotence
Leviticus	Communion and fellowship	Holiness
Numbers	Redirection	Justice
Deuteronomy	Instruction	Faithfulness

CHRONOLOGY OF PERSIAN KINGS RELATED TO THE OLD TESTAMENT

King	Dates (all BC)	Chapters in Ezra	Other Books
Cyrus	538–530	1:1–4:5	
Cambyses	530–522		
Smerdis	522		
Darius I	521–486	5–6	Haggai (520), Zechariah (520–515)
Xerxes I (Ahasuerus)	486–465	4:6	Esther (474)
Artaxerxes I	464–423	4:7–23; 7–10	Malachi (450–400), Nehemiah (445–425)
Darius II			

CHRONOLOGY OF PROPHETS

	Ninth Century BC Prophets	Eighth Century BC Prophets	Seventh and Sixth Century BC Prophets	Exilic Prophets	Postexilic Prophets
Israel		Jonah Amos Hosea			
Judah	Obadiah Joel	Isaiah Micah	Nahum Zephaniah Habakkuk Jeremiah	Daniel Ezekiel	Haggai Zechariah Malachi

Assyrian Exile of Israel 722 BC

Babylonian Exile of Judah 586 BC

THE KINGS AND PROPHETS[11]

THE NORTHERN KINGDOM: ISRAEL 931–722 BC			
Kings	**Godly?**	**Years Reigned**	**Scripture Record**
Jeroboam I	No	22	1 Kings 12–14
Nadab	No	2	1 Kings 15
Baasha	No	24	1 Kings 15–16
Elah	No	2	1 Kings 16
Zimri	No	7 days	1 Kings 16
Omri	No	12	1 Kings 16
Ahab	No	22	1 Kings 16–22
Ahaziah	No	2	1 Kings 22; 2 Kings 1
Jehoram (Joram)	No	12	2 Kings 3–8
Jehu	No	28	2 Kings 9–10
Jehoahaz (Joahaz)	No	17	2 Kings 13
Jehoash (Joash)	No	16	2 Kings 13
Jeroboam II	No	41	2 Kings 14
Zechariah	No	6 months	2 Kings 15
Shallum	No	1 month	2 Kings 15
Menahem	No	10	2 Kings 15
Pekahiah	No	2	2 Kings 15
Pekah	No	20	2 Kings 15
Hoshea	No	9	2 Kings 17

Prophets (side labels): ELIJAH (Ahab–Jehoram), ELISHA (Jehu–Jehoash), HOSEA (Jeroboam II–Hoshea); JONAH and AMOS (Jeroboam II)

THE KINGS AND PROPHETS[11]

The Southern Kingdom: Judah 931–586 BC

	Kings	Godly?	Years Reigned	Scripture Record
	Rehoboam	No	17	1 Kings 12–14; 2 Chron. 11–12
	Abijah (Abijam)	No	3	1 Kings 15; 2 Chron. 13
	Asa	Yes	41	1 Kings 15; 2 Chron. 14–16
	Jehoshaphat	Yes	25	1 Kings 22; 2 Chron. 17–20
Obadiah	Jehoram	No	8	2 Kings 8; 2 Chron. 21
	Ahaziah	No	1	2 Kings 8; 2 Chron. 22
	Queen Athaliah	No	6	2 Kings 11; 2 Chron. 22–23
Joel	Joash (Jehoash)	Yes	40	2 Kings 12–13; 2 Chron. 24
	Amaziah	Yes	29	2 Kings 14; 2 Chron. 25
	Uzziah (Azariah)	Yes	52	2 Kings 15; 2 Chron. 26
Micah, Isaiah	Jotham	Yes	16	2 Kings 15; 2 Chron. 27
Micah, Isaiah	Ahaz	No	16	2 Kings 16; 2 Chron. 28; Isa.7–12
Micah, Isaiah	Hezekiah	Yes	29	2 Kings 18–20; 2 Chron. 29–32; Isa. 36–39
Isaiah, Nahum	Manasseh	No	55	2 Kings 21; 2 Chron. 33
	Amon	No	2	2 Kings 21; 2 Chron. 33
Jeremiah, Zephaniah	Josiah	Yes	31	2 Kings 22–23; 2 Chron. 34–35
Jeremiah	Jehoahaz (Joahaz)	No	3 months	2 Kings 23; 2 Chron. 36
Jeremiah, Habakkuk	Jehoiakim	No	11	2 Kings 23–24; 2 Chron. 36
Jeremiah	Jehoiachin	No	3 months	2 Kings 24; 2 Chron. 36
Jeremiah	Zedekiah	No	11	2 Kings 24–25; 2 Chron. 36; Jer. 52

THE THREE RETURNS FROM EXILE* 12

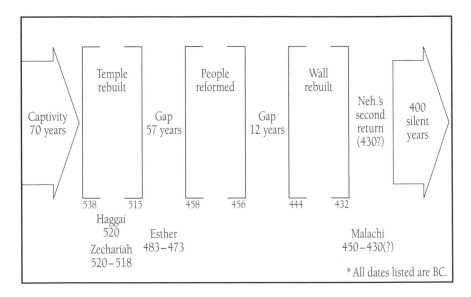

Captivity 70 years

Temple rebuilt

Gap 57 years

People reformed

Gap 12 years

Wall rebuilt

Neh.'s second return (430?)

400 silent years

538   515   458   456   444   432

Haggai
520
Zechariah
520–518

Esther
483–473

Malachi
450–430(?)

* All dates listed are BC.

COMPARING THE GOSPELS

	Matthew	Mark	Luke	John
Portrayal of Jesus	Messianic King	Suffering Servant	Son of Man	Son of God
Primary Recipients	Jews	Roman church	Theophilus and all Gentiles	All people
Primary Purpose	To show Jesus as Israel's long-awaited Messiah	To strengthen suffering believers by focusing on the suffering yet triumphant Savior	To provide a warm, human portrait of the Savior of the whole world	To encourage belief in the eternal Son of God
Probable Order of Writing	Second	First	Third	Fourth
Material Shared with Other Gospels	58%	93%	41%	8%

THE BOOK OF PHILIPPIANS

A Study of Philippians

Author: Paul   Date: circa AD 62

There is	Joy in Living	Joy in Serving	Joy in Sharing	Joy in Resting
	• when we don't get what we want • in spite of circumstances • even with conflicts	• starts with right attitude • maintained through right theology • encouraged by right models	• a warning • a testimony • a goal • a command	• knees • mind • action • faith
	Chapter 1	Chapter 2	Chapter 3	Chapter 4
Christ	. . . My Life	. . . My Model	. . . My Goal	. . . My Contentment
Spirit	His Provision (1:19)	His Fellowship (2:1)	His Worship (3:3)	His Peace (4:7)
Positive Reaction	To Difficulty *Now I want you to know, brethren, that my circumstances have turned out for the greater progress of the gospel.* (1:12)	To Others *Do all things without grumbling or disputing.* (2:14)	To the Past *Forgetting what lies behind and reaching forward to what lies ahead, I press on toward the goal for the prize of the upward call of God in Christ Jesus.* (3:13–14)	To the "Unchangeables" *Not that I speak from want, for I have learned to be content in whatever circumstances I am.* (4:11)
Tone	Warm, encouraging, affirming			
Key Words	"Rejoice," "Christ," "Mind," "Act"			
Uniqueness	• No major problem passages • "Joy" is found in each chapter • Not one quotation from the Old Testament		• Christ mentioned over forty times • Most positive of all Paul's letters, yet written while he was chained to a Roman guard	
Key Verse	For to me, to live is Christ and to die is gain. (Philippians 1:21)			

HOW TO BEGIN A
RELATIONSHIP WITH GOD

The world is filled with competing theories about God, religion, and salvation. Alternate views of Jesus vie for our attention at every turn. Different paths to different gods market themselves in the ever-changing desert of ideas. Yet in the midst of this world of contradictory claims, Jesus Christ made a bold assertion: "I am the way, and the truth, and the life; no one comes to the Father but through Me" (John 14:6).

In a confusing world filled with signs pointing us down different roads of philosophies and religions, can we be sure we've placed our feet on the right path? The answer to this question comes from the all-time best-selling book, translated into more languages and read by more people than any other book in human history. The Bible alone clearly marks the way of truth and salvation with four vital markers.

Our Spiritual Condition: Totally Depraved

The first marker is rather personal. One look in the mirror of Scripture, and our human condition becomes painfully clear:

> There is none righteous, not even one;
> There is none who understands,
> There is none who seeks for God;
> All have turned aside, together they have become
> useless;
> There is none who does good,
> There is not even one. (Romans 3:10–12)

We are all sinners through and through—totally depraved, completely corrupt. Now, that doesn't mean we've committed every atrocity known to humankind. We're not as *bad* as we can be, just as *bad off* as we can be. Sin colors all our thoughts, motives, words, and actions.

You still don't believe it? Look around. Everything in this broken world bears the smudge marks of our sinful nature. Despite our best efforts to create a paradise on earth, crime statistics continue to soar, divorce rates keep climbing, and families keep crumbling.

Something has gone terribly wrong in our society and in ourselves, something deadly. Contrary to how the world would repackage it, "me first" living doesn't equal rugged individuality and freedom; it equals death. As Paul said in his letter to the Romans, "The wages of sin is death" (Romans 6:23)—our emotional and physical death through sin's destructiveness, and our spiritual death from God's righteous judgment of our sin. This brings us to the second marker: God's character.

God's Character: Infinitely Holy

When he observed the condition of the world and the people in it, the wise King Solomon concluded, "Vanity of vanities! All is vanity" (Ecclesiastes 1:2; 12:8). The fact that we know things are not as they should be points us to a standard of goodness beyond ourselves. Our sense of injustice in life implies a perfect standard of justice. That standard and source is God Himself. And God's standard of holiness contrasts starkly with our sinful condition.

Scripture says that "God is Light, and in Him there is no darkness at all" (1 John 1:5). He is absolutely holy—which creates a problem for us. If He is so pure, how can we who are so impure relate to Him?

Perhaps we could try being better people, try to tilt the balance in favor of our good deeds, or seek out wisdom and knowledge for self-improvement. Throughout history, people have attempted to live up to God's standard by keeping the Ten Commandments or by living out their own code of ethics. Unfortunately, no one can come close to satisfying the demands of God's law. Romans 3:20 says, "By the works of the Law no flesh will be justified in His sight; for through the Law comes the knowledge of sin."

Our Need: A Substitute

So here we are, sinners by nature, sinners by choice, trying to pull ourselves up by our own bootstraps and attain a relationship with our holy Creator. But every time we try, we fall flat on our faces. We can't live a good enough life to make up for our sin, because God's standard isn't "good enough"—it's perfection. And we can't make amends for the offense our sin has created without dying for it.

Who can get us out of this mess?

If someone could live perfectly, honoring God's law, and would bear sin's death penalty for us—in our place—then we would be saved from our predicament. But is there such a person? Thankfully, yes!

Meet your substitute—*Jesus Christ*. He is the One who took death's place for you!

> [God] made [Jesus Christ] who knew no sin to be sin on our behalf, so that we might become the righteousness of God in Him. (2 Corinthians 5:21)

God's Provision: A Savior

God rescued us by sending His Son, Jesus, to die on the cross for our sins (1 John 4:9–10). Jesus was fully human and fully divine (John 1:1, 14), a truth that ensures His understanding of our weaknesses, His power to forgive, and His ability to bridge the gap between God and us (Romans 5:6–11). In short, we are "justified as a gift by His grace through the redemption which is in Christ Jesus" (Romans 3:24). Two words in this verse bear further explanation: *justified* and *redemption*.

Justification is God's act of mercy, in which He declares believing sinners righteous, while they are still in their sinning state. Justification doesn't mean that God *makes* us righteous so that we never sin again; rather, He *declares* us righteous—much like a judge pardons a guilty criminal. Because Jesus took our sin upon Himself and suffered our judgment on the cross, God forgives our debt and proclaims us PARDONED.

Redemption is God's act of paying the ransom price to release us from our bondage to sin. Held hostage by Satan, we were shackled by the iron chains of sin and death. Like a loving parent whose child has been kidnapped, God willingly paid the ransom for you. And what a price He paid! He gave His only Son to bear our sins—past, present, and future. Jesus's death and resurrection broke our chains and set us free to become children of God (Romans 6:16–18, 22; Galatians 4:4–7).

Placing Your Faith in Christ

These four markers pointing us to the way of truth describe how God has provided a way to Himself through Jesus Christ. Because the price has been paid in full by God, we must respond to His free gift of eternal life in total faith and confidence in Him to save us. We must step forward into the relationship with God that He has prepared for us—not by doing good works or being a good person but by coming to Him just as we are and accepting His justification and redemption by faith.

> For by grace you have been saved through faith; and that not of yourselves, it is the gift of God; not as a result of works, so that no one may boast. (Ephesians 2:8–9)

We accept God's gift of salvation simply by placing our faith in Christ alone for the forgiveness of our sins. Would you like to enter a relationship with your Creator by trusting in Christ as your Savior? If so, here's a simple prayer you can use to express your faith:

> *Dear God,*
>
> *I know that my sin has put a barrier between You and me. Thank You for sending Your Son, Jesus, to die in my place. I trust in Jesus alone to forgive my sins, and I accept His gift of eternal life. I ask Jesus to be my personal Savior and the Lord of my life. Thank You. In Jesus's name, amen.*

If you've prayed this prayer or one like it and you wish to find out more about knowing God and His plan for you in the Bible, contact us at Insight for Living. You can contact one of our pastors on staff by using the information below.

Of all the relationships you enjoy in this life, none can compare with a relationship with God through Jesus Christ, who loved us and gave Himself for us. That first step by faith onto the true path begins a personal and eternal relationship with God.

Insight for Living
Pastoral Ministries Department
Post Office Box 269000
Plano, Texas 75026-9000
(972) 473-5097, Monday through Friday,
8:00 a.m. – 5:00 p.m. Central time
www.insight.org/contactapastor

WE ARE HERE FOR YOU

If you desire to find out more about knowing God and His plan for you in the Bible, contact us. Insight for Living provides staff pastors and women's counselors who are available for free written correspondence or phone consultation. These seminary-trained and seasoned men and women have years of pastoral experience and are well-qualified guides for your spiritual journey.

Please feel welcome to contact our Pastoral Ministries department by using the information below:

Insight for Living
Pastoral Ministries Department
Post Office Box 269000
Plano, Texas 75026-9000
(972) 473-5097, Monday through Friday,
8:00 a.m. – 5:00 p.m. Central time
www.insight.org/contactapastor

ENDNOTES

1. Chapter adapted from Charles R. Swindoll, "God's Book — God's Voice," in *The Living Insights Study Bible*, gen. ed. Charles R. Swindoll (Grand Rapids: Zondervan, 1996), 1312–15. Used by permission.

2. Wayne Stiles, "The Benefits of Understanding and Experiencing the Historical Geography of Israel" (D.Min. diss., Dallas Theological Seminary, 2004), 76. Used by permission.

3. Chapter adapted from Wayne Stiles, *Going Places with God: A Devotional Journey through the Lands of the Bible* (Ventura, Calif.: Regal, 2006), 26, 107, 162–65. Used by permission.

4. Martin Luther, *Werke*, Erl. Frkf. ed., vol. LXIV, 382, quoted in Philip Schaff, *History of the Christian Church*, vol. VII, *Modern Christianity: The German Reformation* (Grand Rapids: Eerdmans, 1950), 305n1. Translation by Michael J. Svigel.

5. Clement, *1 Clement* 45.2–3, in *The Apostolic Fathers: Greek Texts and English Translations*, updated ed., ed. and rev. Michael W. Holmes (Grand Rapids: Baker Books, 1999), 79.

6. Irenaeus, *Against Heresies* 2.27.2, in *Ante-Nicene Fathers: The Writings of the Fathers Down to A.D. 325*, ed. Alexander Roberts, James Donaldson, and A. Cleveland Coxe, vol. 1, *The Apostolic Fathers, Justin Martyr, Irenaeus*, American reprint ed. (Peabody, Mass.: Hendrickson, 1995), 398.

7. Athanasius, *Festal Letter* 39.6, in *Nicene and Post-Nicene Fathers: A Select Library of the Christian Church*, ed. Philip Schaff and Henry Wace, second series, vol. 4, *Athanasius: Selected Works and Letters*, reprint ed. (Peabody, Mass.: Hendrickson, 1995), 552.

8. Martin Luther, "Eight Sermons at Wittenberg, 1522," in *Luther's Works*, ed. and trans. John W. Doberstein, vol. 51, *Sermons I*, gen. ed. Helmut T. Lehmann (Philadelphia: Muhlenberg Press, 1959), 77.

9. John Calvin, *Institutes of the Christian Religion* 1.7.2, trans. Henry Beveridge (Grand Rapids: Eerdmans, 1994), 69.

10. Chart by Bruce Wilkinson and Kenneth Boa, *Talk Thru the New Testament, Volume II* of *Talk Thru the Bible* (Nashville: Thomas Nelson, 1983), 515. Used by permission of Thomas Nelson, Inc.

11. Chart adapted from John F. Walvoord and Roy B. Zuck, eds., *The Bible Knowledge Commentary: Old Testament* (Wheaton, Ill.: Victor, 1985), 513. Copyright © 1985 Cook Communications Ministries. Copied with permission. May not be further reproduced. All rights reserved.

12. Walvoord and Zuck, eds., *The Bible Knowledge Commentary: Old Testament*, 652. Copyright © 1985 Cook Communications Ministries. Copied with permission. May not be further reproduced. All rights reserved.

RESOURCES FOR DIGGING DEEPER

Surgeons need scalpels. Builders need tool belts. Fishermen need tackle boxes. Anybody who is serious about a calling or career is sure to have the right tools and to know how to use them. That's why Christians who are committed to studying God's Word need well-chosen tools. But how many resources do you need? If you look at the library of Mrs. Johnson, the seasoned Christian who has been reading the Bible for fifty years, you might conclude that you need a yard or two. If you inspect your pastor's office, however, you'll find that it can take ten or twenty yards. Visit a seminary professor, and you'll begin to wonder if it takes a football-field's worth!

But the key to being well-equipped for fruitful Bible study is not so much the quantity of tools you have but the quality and kind. Below you'll find a list of resources we recommend for your use as you begin studying the treasure of God's Word.

History

Bingham, D. Jeffrey. *Pocket History of the Church*. Downers Grove, Ill.: InterVarsity, 2002.

Bruce, F. F. *The Canon of Scripture*. Downers Grove, Ill.: InterVarsity, 1988.

Bruce, F. F. *The New Testament Documents: Are They Reliable?* 6th ed. Grand Rapids: Eerdmans, 2003.

Bruce, F. F. *New Testament History*. New York: Doubleday, 1971.

Gonzalez, Justo L. *The Story of Christianity: The Early Church to the Dawn of the Reformation*. Vol. 1. San Francisco: HarperSanFrancisco, 1984.

Gonzalez, Justo L. *The Story of Christianity: The Reformation to the Present Day*. Vol. 2. San Francisco: HarperSanFrancisco, 1985.

Packer, J. I., and Merrill C. Tenney. *Manners and Customs of Bible Times.* Nashville: Thomas Nelson, 2003.

Shelley, Bruce L. *Church History in Plain Language.* Updated 2d ed. Waco, Tex.: Word, 1995.

Svigel, Michael J. *Heroes and Heretics: Solving the Modern Mystery of the Ancient Church.* Plano, Tex.: IFL Publishing House, 2006.

Bible Commentaries

Bailey, Mark, and Tom Constable. *The New Testament Explorer: Discovering the Essence, Background, and Meaning of Every Book in the New Testament.* Nashville: Word, 1999.

Barker, Kenneth L., and John R. Kohlenberger III. *The Expositor's Bible Commentary.* Abridged ed. Grand Rapids: Zondervan, 2004.

Dyer, Charles H., and Gene Merrill. *The Old Testament Explorer: Discovering the Essence, Background, and Meaning of Every Book in the Old Testament.* Nashville: Word, 2001.

Radmacher, Earl, Ronald B. Allen, and H. Wayne House. *Nelson's New Illustrated Bible Commentary.* Nashville: Thomas Nelson, 1999.

Walvoord, John F., and Roy B. Zuck. *The Bible Knowledge Commentary.* Wheaton, Ill.: Victor Books, 1985.

Wiersbe, Warren W. *The Bible Exposition Commentary.* Vols. 1–5. Colorado Springs: Cook Communications, 2004.

Bible Dictionaries

Douglas, J. D., and Merrill C. Tenney, eds. *The New International Dictionary of the Bible.* Pictorial ed. Grand Rapids: Zondervan, 1987.

Unger, Merrill F. *The New Unger's Bible Dictionary.* Chicago: Moody Publishers, 2006.

Unger, Merrill F. *The New Unger's Bible Handbook.* Ed. and rev. by Gary J. Larson. Chicago: Moody Publishers, 2005.

Vine, W. E. *Vine's Expository Dictionary of Old and New Testament Words.* Nashville: Thomas Nelson, 2003.

Bible Study

Hendricks, Howard G., and William D. Hendricks. *Living by the Book.* Chicago: Moody Press, 1993.

Kreeft, Peter. *You Can Understand the Bible: A Practical and Illuminating Guide to Each Book in the Bible.* Fort Collins, Colo.: Ignatius Press, 2005.

Ryken, Leland. *How to Read the Bible as Literature.* Grand Rapids: Zondervan, Academie Books, 1984.

Stott, John R. W. *Understanding the Bible.* Exp. ed. Grand Rapids: Zondervan, 1999.

Zuck, Roy B. *Basic Bible Interpretation: A Practical Guide to Understanding Biblical Truth.* Colorado Springs: Chariot Victor, 1999.

Geography/Archaeology

Beitzel, Barry J. *The Moody Atlas of Bible Lands.* Chicago: Moody Press, 1985.

Brisco, Thomas C. *Holman Bible Atlas: A Complete Guide to the Expansive Geography of Biblical History.* Nashville: Broadman & Holman, 1998.

Dyer, Charles H., and Gregory A. Hatteberg. *Christian Traveler's Guide to the Holy Land.* Nashville: Broadman & Holman, 1998.

Free, Joseph P. *Archaeology and Bible History.* Rev. and exp. by Howard F. Vos. Grand Rapids: Zondervan, 1992.

Laney, J. Carl. *Baker's Concise Bible Atlas: A Geographical Study of Bible History.* Grand Rapids: Baker Book House, 1988.

Rasmussen, Carl G. *The Zondervan NIV Atlas of the Bible.* Grand Rapids: Zondervan, 1999.

Stiles, Wayne. *Going Places with God: A Devotional Journey through the Lands of the Bible.* Ventura, Calif.: Regal, 2006.

Wilson, Neil S., and Linda K. Taylor. *Tyndale Handbook of Bible Charts and Maps*. Wheaton, Ill.: Tyndale House, 2001.

Theology

Insight for Living. *Growing Deep in the Christian Life: Returning to Our Roots Workbook*. Plano, Tex.: IFL Publishing House, 2005.

Insight for Living. *The Way of Truth in a World of Fiction: Beyond the Da Vinci Code*. Plano, Tex.: IFL Publishing House, 2006.

Little, Paul E. *Know What You Believe*. Rev. and exp. ed. Colorado Springs: Cook Communications, 2003.

Lutzer, Erwin W. *Seven Reasons Why You Can Trust the Bible*. Chicago: Moody, 2001.

McDowell, Josh. *The New Evidence that Demands a Verdict*. Rev. and updated ed. Nashville: Thomas Nelson, 1999.

Ryrie, Charles. *Basic Theology: A Popular Systematic Guide to Understanding Biblical Truth*. Chicago: Moody Publishers, 1999.

Stott, John R. W. *Basic Christianity*. Rev. ed. Grand Rapids: Eerdmans, 1986.

Strobel, Lee. *The Case for Christ: A Journalist's Personal Investigation of the Evidence for Jesus*. Grand Rapids: Zondervan, 1998.

Swindoll, Charles R. *Growing Deep in the Christian Life: Returning to Our Roots*. Grand Rapids: Zondervan, 1995.

Swindoll, Charles R., and Roy B. Zuck, eds. *Understanding Christian Theology*. Nashville: Thomas Nelson, 2003.

Electronic Tools

Accordance is a powerful Bible research and reference tool for the Mac platform. It includes searchable Greek and Hebrew texts, translations, and can be expanded with additional electronic resources. It is available online at www.accordancebible.com.

BibleWorks is a software program for the PC platform that allows users to cross-reference among many different Bible versions in many different languages, including Greek and Hebrew. It also contains a variety of commentaries and other resources. It is available online at www.bibleworks.com.

Bible.org. This evangelical Web site hosts not only the NET Bible but also countless articles on biblical studies as well as theological and current topics. Access is free at www.bible.org.

Christian Classics Ethereal Library. This is an online collection of historical writings in the public domain. Access is free, and their collection is quite extensive. It can be accessed at www.ccel.org.

Logos software is a combination of Bible commentaries, Bible dictionaries and encyclopedias, and other Bible study resources. It is available for a variety of educational and interest levels, from the "Christian Home Library" to the "Scholar's Library." It is available at www.logos.com.

ABOUT THE AUTHORS

Charles R. Swindoll

Chancellor of Dallas Theological Seminary and best-selling author, Chuck also serves as pastor of Stonebriar Community Church in Frisco, Texas, where he's able to do what he loves most — teach the Bible to willing hearts. His focus on practical Bible application has been heard on the *Insight for Living* radio broadcast since 1979.

John Adair

John Adair is a writer in the Creative Ministries department of Insight for Living. He received his bachelor's degree from Criswell College and his Master of Theology degree from Dallas Theological Seminary, where he is currently completing his Ph.D. in Historical Theology. He resides in the Dallas area with his wife, Laura, and their two children.

Derrick G. Jeter

Derrick serves as a creative writer for Insight for Living. A graduate of Dallas Theological Seminary, Derrick's passion is to exhort believers to understand and apply the Scriptures and to engage unbelievers with the truth of Christ's death and resurrection. Derrick lives in the Dallas area with his wife, Christy, and their five children.

Wil Luce

A graduate of Dallas Theological Seminary, Wil has served with Insight for Living since 1987 as a pastoral counselor. From his home in California, Wil oversees Insight for Living's correspondence ministry to prison inmates. He and his wife, Diane, have four grown children and five grandchildren.

Barb Peil

As a staff writer and managing editor, Barb contributed to Insight for Living from 1994 to 2002. A graduate of Dallas Theological Seminary, she also served as an adjunct instructor at Biola University. She currently works as the director of communications for a Christian ministry in Illinois.

Wendy Peterson

Wendy Peterson served with Insight for Living from 1986 through 2002 in the Pastoral Ministries department as an editor and assistant study guide writer. Wendy holds a B.A. in Communications from California State University, Fullerton, and she has been involved in numerous freelance writing and editing projects, including online education courses.

Wayne Stiles

After serving in the pastorate for fourteen years, Wayne joined the staff at Insight for Living and currently serves as executive vice president. He received his Master of Theology and Doctor of Ministry degrees from Dallas Theological Seminary. Wayne and his wife, Cathy, have two teenage daughters.

Michael J. Svigel

Michael has been writing for Insight for Living since 2004. He is a graduate of Dallas Theological Seminary, where he received his Master of Theology in New Testament and completed his Ph.D. work in Theological Studies. Mike lives in the Dallas area with his wife, Stephanie, and their three children.

ORDERING INFORMATION

If you would like to order additional copies of the *Insight's Bible Handbook* or to order other Insight for Living resources, please contact the office that serves you.

United States

Insight for Living
Post Office Box 269000
Plano, Texas 75026-9000
USA
1-800-772-8888 (Monday through Thursday, 7:00 a.m. – 9:00 p.m., and Friday, 7:00 a.m. – 7:00 p.m. Central time)
www.insight.org

Canada

Insight for Living Canada
Post Office Box 2510
Vancouver, BC V6B 3W7
CANADA
1-800-663-7639
www.insightforliving.ca

Australia, New Zealand, and South Pacific

Insight for Living Australia
Post Office Box 1011
Bayswater, VIC 3153
AUSTRALIA
1 300 467 444
www.insight.asn.au

United Kingdom and Europe

Insight for Living United Kingdom
Post Office Box 348
Leatherhead
KT22 2DS
UNITED KINGDOM
0800 915 9364
www.insightforliving.org.uk

Other International Locations

International constituents may contact the U.S. office through our Web
site (www.insight.org), mail queries, or by calling +1-972-473-5136.